This book is dedicated to my **98-year-old** gorgeous grandmother **Armer Lee** who has wisdom etched in the crevices of her perfectly chiseled face. You are my inspiration and I am grateful to God for allowing me to experience His amazing grace through you!

Dedicated also to the ladies of **STEM** for exposing past pains to heal the hurts of wounded women and men around the world…TV, Erin and Fatima.

BEYOND BLESSED

*Distractions Have a Name
and Purpose Has a Face*

MAURA GALE

**Foreword By
Dr. Kimberly Leslie-Patton**

Immaculate Conceptions Publishing Company
In association with
Gathering House Publishing

Beyond Blessed
Distractions Have a Name and Purpose Has a Face
Maura Gale
PO Box 366001, Atlanta, GA 30336

Cover Design by: Kevin Allen of KA Designs

ISBN: 978-0-9743811-1-X   0 2 0 9 1 7
10 9 8
Printed in the United States of America

♾ This paper meets the requirements of ANSI/NISO Z39.48-1992
(Permanence of Paper)

Summary of My Insides

'A Piece Of Peace' is shared after every chapter as spiritual insight and understanding for the life lessons learned.

Acknowledgements

I thank God the Father, Son and Holy Spirit for entrusting me with these life lessons and experiences as well as the opportunity to articulate them accurately, openly and honestly. I will forever yield my pen to you!

Thank you Mommy for your sacrifices, ambition and tenacity. Your example promotes my productivity. Your generosity, strength and focus forced me to move forward!

Thank you Dunn (Daddy). Your constant commitment in communicating and conveying your love for me has been one of my greatest gifts.

To my immediate family, my 12 nieces and nephews, all relatives and the fabulous fans I'm blessed to have…thank you for the continued support and encouragement to write, do and be who God designed me to be! A special thanks to my Chi Town cuz'ns Kim & Lynn, Philly cuz'ns Kenny & Darlene and Hot-Lanta cuz'ns Rose and Keenan.

To Artisha (TT) and James Randall my niece and nephew who always reach out to hollah at me in Cali…thanks.

To my uncles JT, Roy, LD, Doug and Rayford and my aunts Margaret, Chris, Annette, Alberta, Annie your belief in my talents blesses me.

Thanks to my creative consultant cousins in B'ham Kim, Ralph, Kerri, Jeh and Cousin Andrew in Montgomery, also DJ Strick and LaShanna (my 2 honorary cousins☺) I love you guys beyond words.

Millie Culver (mom-in-love) for infinite reasons!

TV Blake for your eagle eyes on the first draft.

The breakfast posse (Lana-Lana and Mayo-naise) without our brain storming sessions my pen would have been dried up a long time ago...I love ya'll!

Falana for an incredible job editing and encouraging me to keep my deadlines, this would not have happened without your dedication!

Thank you to the Chef's who seasoned my SOUL'S FOOD.

Bishop Eddie Long, Bishop Arthur Brazier, Bishop Kenneth Ulmer.

A special thank you to the Pastors, church groups and organizations that have extended a warm invitation for me to share my testimony and talents with God's people.

A special thanks to the fuel for my fire...my friends

TDP, Hal Martin, Arienne, "Reece Cup," Melanie, Falana, Sondra, McClinton, Delores & The Sista Girls, Mo Poetic, Yolanda C, Candace, Malvena, Samuel, Mela Lee, Side 2 Side, Samantha, Shawndra, Shandle, Debbie, Faune, Miss Kimm, Chuck G. and DET.

Foreword
Dr. Kimberly Leslie-Patton

This riveting message of truth restores and renews your faith, transforms your vision and propels you to have walking on water faith, because you know with confidence that your better days are ahead.

This honest, real life, fast paced, prime time drama on the stage of life - results in daily VICTORY and TRIUMPH despite the challenges, trials and distractions. *Beyond Blessed* will change, confront and transform your journey – take you to the mountain to face the reality of life's obstacles so that you hear the voice of the Spirit as he leads you to new heights to boldly speak and miraculously see with renewed vision, your faith in action.

Your past will no longer hold you bound. Today, expect your hurts and pains to be healed by the power of the words and anointing contained in this book. Anticipate that you will have renewed speech, and plans to achieve your beyond blessed life. Your willingness to take a journey into transparency will propel you to the awareness that you too, can reach your potential and purpose in life and realize with renewed attentiveness, the value of your abundantly blessed life.

Maura Gale's gift is revolutionary and empowering. She sincerely shares recollections of life's challenging realities in an honest way. *Beyond Blessed* will change a generation. It takes the mask off the things that we have too long sat in silence about. We perish for lack of knowledge – no more!

This book raises the awareness of distractions and it doesn't matter what the attraction to the distraction is, you will be set free to walk and talk in liberty and freedom. It will break the yokes and bondages from your mind, heart, soul, spirit, and emotions, leading you to the feet of Jesus. There He removes the stain of your past and loves you back to a life filled with peace, joy, and an earnest expectation that you can rise up and live *Beyond Blessed*. The Truth shall definitely set your free this day. Believe it. Receive it. Live the *Beyond Blessed* life.

Maura Gale takes you on a journey full of valleys and hills to 'HOLYwood'. As you go down memory lane in laughter as well as tears of joy and sorrow, you will read of God's restorative power. She opens the eyes of your understanding with practical reminders of His love, mercy and righteousness. Prepare to reflect upon the price of the oil in your vessel – see just how valuable you are and go walk and talk in the abundance of blessings and benefits that God makes available to you this day and forever. I decree, confess, profess, and command that you live the *Beyond Blessed* life from this day forward.

Dr. Kimberly Leslie-Patton
Leslie Patton & Associates
Author of the soon to be released book and recording
" Journey's End"
Check the website for release date.
KimLPatton@gmail.com
www.lesliepattonandassociates.com

Introduction

It's my hope that if you are reading this book you are open to embracing change, uncovering old wounds and analyzing foundational pivot points and/or detours in your life. My goal is to share with you some real life examples - of how I grew up, what types of challenges I endured, some mistakes I've made, the disappointments I've encountered, and several of the set backs I've caused. It's impossible to get to the center or core of you without peeling off the layers of protection that we ourselves put in place. Having said that, I pray my transparency reveals rays of hope, while the spiritual insights I share take you on a journey down a stream that leads to God's ocean of promises. Because that's how vast and wide His promises are! Once you can conceive that reality you are on your way to living BEYOND BLESSED.

Have you ever thought about how God views you? When you look at yourself and your life, what image or perception comes to mind? We've all made mistakes and knowingly said and done things that were contrary to God's word. However, a distorted picture embedded in your mind can cause you to short circuit God's clear description.

What if, I could help you visualize God's View of YOU? What if, I could paint a picture with words...God's words to encourage you along your journey in life? Would you change your perception about yourself or would you at best wish, hope and pray it were true? My desire is to reveal the reality of God's view of you and to make the image and description so practical and applicable until there is no room to doubt how God sees you.

I'll start with myself to show how against all odds I managed to make an exodus from what could be thought of as hell on earth. Don't be deceived; all of my trials led me on a trail to trust... I now trust God. God has turned my mourning into dancing *(Psalm 30:11),* and given me beauty for ashes *(Isaiah 61:3).* He has seen me at my absolute worst - and He still calls me His. What continuously blows my mind is that in spite of my shortcomings He loves me and desires to bless me. Now brace yourself for the bumpy beauty of honesty being exposed through me...to reveal the real you.

"Beyond Blessed"

Distractions Have A Name
&
Purpose Has A Face

Beyond (bi-yond)
1. More or better than; in addition to; exceeding
2. Something that lies outside the scope of ordinary

Blessed (bless-'id)
1. Consecrated, sacred, sanctified
2. Worthy of adoration, reverence or worship
3. Favored, fortunate

You are:
More than Favored
Better than Fortunate
Worthy of Adoration
Outside of Ordinary

BEYOND BLESSED!

Chapter 1

The Root Of It

The past can propel you to
purpose but it does not dictate it.

Around the tender age of 6 I remember watching "Leave it to Beaver," "The Brady Bunch" and "The Walton's" on TV. I saw mothers and fathers living in the same house, having family time with their kids, and eating meals together and passing food while laughing and talking. In the evening they would all sit on the front porch and the mother would sip lemonade or iced tea, and the father would read his newspaper while the kids played safely in the front yard.

However, in the world of the ghetto, you see a totally different show. The matrix of your mind becomes your reality because you only witness a world that's closed, chaotic, and combative. If you grow up watching ladies of the night on every corner, walls laced with graffiti, streets covered with broken wine bottles, and drug dealers driving around looking for a new customer you could potentially grow up believing that's all there is to life. But if you move outside of your mile and a half radius of reality and into the real world, you realize there's much more to life than back yards full of concrete, stale stinky smells that suffocate the air, and creepy crawlers called cockroaches that basically set up camp inside yo' crib.

Welcome to my world… the ghetto!

I was born and raised in Chicago, Illinois. There was 6 ½ of us, my mother, my 3 sisters, my older brother, my part-time daddy and me. We were crammed in a small 3 bedroom, 1 bath apartment. All of the bedrooms were located upstairs. I grew up on the south side in a housing project called Altgeld Gardens. There were worse projects in Chicago, but one thing all projects had in common was each community had about a 12-block radius of existence. The inner city was exactly that, *an inside city*. You never had to go outside of the area for anything. There was a drug store, some liquor stores, a currency exchange, a grocery store, a free clinic, a school, and an unreliable bus line. Everything you needed was within walking distance with the exception of a *bank*, a *hospital*, a *police station* and a *department store*.

All the apartments in Altgeld looked just alike. They each had a raggedy screen door and a one-step front porch with a concrete awning. Some of the front yards were nice, but most were full of dirt and some weeds. Behind the apartments was low-to-no maintenance concrete. Inside our place were creepy crawling critters. Now I'm not talking about pets - I'm talking about pests, cockroaches and water bugs to be more exact. I would see a whole lot of them if someone moved in or out on my block. They were so bad they'd take control of our apartment at nighttime and sometimes I'd find them crawling on me in my sleep. If I woke up in the middle of the night to get a glass of water, when I turned the light on in the kitchen there would be turmoil and disarray. It was as if 'light' was some kind of roach signal for 'run'…and when that light hit they would all scatter.

I remember how we always rinsed any dish or glass we removed from the kitchen cabinets before we used them. We never left food sitting out on top of the stove, counters or table. Food was always stored inside the stove or refrigerator until someone re-heated it. To this day I still rinse out my dishes even though I haven't had a problem with bugs since I lived in the ghetto over 20 years ago. Some habits are hard to break.

One of the really cool things about growing up in the ghetto was what I like to call the "wine-o's talent show". Around 5 o'clock, on the weekend older men used to sing songs on the corner while drinking out of a brown paper bag. They sounded so good I'd sit on my front porch and listen to them. However, when they talked I couldn't seem to make out what they said because they slurred their words into sounds. But when they'd sing I would tune in…they sang songs like "Sadie…don't you know I love you sweet Sadie"… Earth Wind and Fire's "Reasons…the reasons why we're here"… "Girl you know I… I…I…I love you" and oooh the Commodores "Because I'm eeeeasy yeah, easy like Sunday morning."

I knew every one of those songs cause my momma used to play them on the weekends and my sisters and me would sing along. We had this wooden floor model stereo component set that opened up on top in the center. It played 45 and 33 records…real wax. I remember learning how to put the arm of the needle on the record. If songs skipped or repeated in the same place momma had a remedy for that, she showed me how to put a penny on the arm to weigh it down so it would move forward and play the rest of the song. Sometimes the sound would be kind of fuzzy because the albums were so old, they were classics. Those were the days when 8 track tapes were in and black and white television sets were common.

In the morning my little sister and I would eat our breakfast out of plastic bowls in front of the semi working big brown console television set. To turn the channel we used pliers because the knobs were broken off. (I know I am not the only one who grew up having to squeeze the handle of pliers to watch your favorite program). If the reception were bad we'd adjust the coat hanger to the left or right until the picture became clear again. The bent wire hanger served as a make shift antenna and was carefully lodged in a silver hole where the broken off antenna used to be. Poverty didn't have an identity in my household because we had everything the neighbors had. I hadn't realized they were poor too.

My mom was a nurse at Cook County hospital and worked the evening shift from 3pm to 11pm so I didn't see her much growing up. We were what you would call today latch key kids. All of my siblings and I we were born two to four years apart, so the eldest usually watched the younger kids.

It was hard for momma to raise all of us without a little help so we received public aid. If you don't know anything about government assistance here's your introduction. We would receive food stamps. Food stamps were the financial support the government provided to help welfare families purchase groceries. Food stamps looked like "play" money. They came in a stapled booklet with colorful hundreds, fifties, twenties, tens and ones. We would tear the dollar amount out of the booklet to pay for merchandise but we could only buy eatable products.

As with all government systems there were loopholes. I remember some of my neighbors selling their food stamps for real money to purchase whatever they wanted. They would buy clothes, pay to get their hair done, and even buy alcohol. I heard some stores don't even accept food stamps. That wasn't the case in the projects -because the stores in the ghetto would have been put out of business if it weren't for food stamps.

We also received subsidized food packages. My favorite was the big block of orange cheese. The government issued big orange block was hard to cut, but it was the best for making grilled cheese sandwiches. And I loved government grilled cheese sandwiches. The cheese would take awhile to melt but when it did, it was good, stringy and chewy. I would almost choke and gag on it sometimes because it was so thick, but that didn't stop me from eating it. Can I get an amen for the orange block? Another kitchen cabinet must have was carnation powdered milk in the red and white box. All we had to do was add water to the white substance and presto - we had milk. We'd put it in a jar and chill it in the fridge. We'd make chocolate milk, eat our cereal with it and we even ate the southern delicatessen 'milk and cornbread'.

Like most folks, I grew up in a dysfunctional family. There was always tension between my parents. They would yell and scream so much that my dad would eventually get fed up and leave. My mom was as sweet as sugar and as sour as vinegar. Sweet because moms greeted everyone with warmth and food, sour because she fussed at my dad all the time. I guess that's why he stayed the night sometimes and other times he went home. As far back as I can remember he always had his own place.

But when he was around they fought and cursed one another out constantly. I thought profanity was normal in all households. So of course I grew up cursing like a sailor. My parents never seemed to get along. It was like a war zone. My dads missing in action moments fueled their drinking. The result was verbal battles that left me upset and terrified. I believe cocktails gave my parents courage to speak their minds without censoring.

The sad thing is, I think that if they would have left the 'courage' alone when they were younger they might have gotten married. I didn't even realize they weren't married until I was much older. To this day they maintain a love/hate relationship. They love each other but hate to be under the same roof.

Growing up, my father gave me the nickname half-pint. Everybody knows, a gallon is too much, a cup is too small but a half-pint is perfect. I was a daddy's girl if ever there was one. My dad worked real hard as a foreman for a meat plant and on the weekends he was a hustler and a gambler. I remember him coming to pick us up to take us to McDonalds, or occasionally to an amusement park.

But I also remember waiting at the windowsill, falling asleep many times, when he didn't show up. On several occasions my dad was MIA. When this happened I would call taverns and bars from a long list of phone numbers that hung by the telephone in the kitchen trying desperately to locate him. After calling about 5 or 6 bars, a bartender would tell me to hold on and he would yell for my dad.

When my dad got to the phone he would slur in a hello and promise he'd make it up to me. I always found a way to believe him.

Needless to say as a child I was disappointed frequently because he broke some promises. That reality plagued many of my relationships. One thing I can say in favor of my dad is he always helped us out financially. I believe he shared money when he had money. However, living a wild life drinking and gambling sometimes translated into monetary and emotional losses.

For the most part my mom was a single parent. I got to give it up to my momma - she made a lot of sacrifices to give us a better life. She sacrificed time with us to work double shifts 3 nights a week and on her off days. She worked hard to save and move us out the projects.

Unfortunately neither my dad nor mom could give me what I needed more than anything, which was time. I believed time-equaled love. I wanted and needed time with them. Consequently, I looked for love in all the wrong places and I grew up believing that promises were meant to be broken.

My mom is a very focused person and she did what she had to do to accomplish her goals. Her hard work paid off because, when I was about 8 years old she purchased a house in a middle class neighborhood and for the first time in my life I felt safe. However, my 4th grade paradise only lasted about a week. The kids found out that I was from the projects and that fact became their ammo to challenge and tease me. I remember the exact incident that started my "street smart mentality." It was September 1975, 3:15 on a Friday afternoon. It was the last day of my first week of school. I was wearing a pretty pink dress (my favorite color) when a girl name Tammy sauntered up to me all cocky. Tammy was the same age as me, bald headed and the only young person I ever knew that wore a wig daily. My momma and some of her friends used to wear wigs but I had never seen a little girl wear one before.

Tammy walked over with her hands on her hips, rolling her neck teasing me about my crooked teeth. That was a sore spot for me because I always wanted braces but momma couldn't afford to get them for me. After dealing with her taunting me all week I was frustrated. I was small for my grade because I started kindergarten at age 4 instead of 5 due to my November birthday coming late in the year, but I was also tough for my size. Tammy and I were in the center of what seemed like 100 kids. They were instigating and egging us on. Tammy had called me project girl and bucktooth one too many times and right about the time I decided I would just smack her in the mouth to shut her up, she pushed me. I fell down on my butt in the dirt but I didn't cry. In the ghetto you had to be tough in all circumstances. By the tender age of 8 I already knew the value of that lesson.

Well needless to say my favorite pink dress got dirty. And since fighting was no stranger to this ghetto fabulous girl, I calmly got up, dusted the back of my dress off, clapped the dirt from my hands, balled up my left fist and punched her right in the nose. I hit her so hard her wig fell off, her nose started bleeding and she ran home crying.

The kids were laughing, teasing her and chanting *"cry baby Tammy…ball headed Tammy…you betta run tell a friend befo' she beat yo butt again"* over and over they screamed it out towards her till she was out of sight. Tammy never picked a fight with me again and neither did any one else from Bennett Elementary.

That day I became second in charge in a schoolyard gang. A white girl name Vicki was the first in charge, the lieutenant. Our gang was sort of harmless, we would lead the kids off the playground during recess to ring doorbells in the neighborhood and run. We would play truth or dare and do double dares, making somebody sneak the ruler off the teachers desk while her back was turned or put chewing gum on someone's seat. One of my personal favorites was to take the toilet paper from a bathroom stall so when someone used the restroom and needed it, they had to drip-dry or go to another stall with their pants down at their ankles.

By 7th grade I was leading the kids off campus on our lunch break taking them to an abandoned bus to smoke Newport cigarettes. The bus was a broken down old yellow school bus with raggedy seats and broken windows. It was parked about a block and a half away from school behind my house on a vacant lot at 100th and Michigan Avenue. The principal, Mr. Long, caught us one day because we got back after the late bell sounded. That stunt cost me a suspension from school for a week.

I was already a mischievous little girl but I learned even more tricks from Vicki - the leader of our little gang and the only kid I knew that could smoke and curse in front of her parents. They actually didn't care. It made no difference to them if she went to school or stayed home. So when we got suspended it wasn't a problem. I forged my moms name on the parent consent form and Vicki and me hung out at her house that whole week smoking cigarettes. It was cool even though her house reeked of cat's piss because they had about 20+ cats. So I ended the 7th grade classified as a cool, popular kid with a very nasty habit… cigarette smoking.

By 8th grade word had gotten around that I was a good kisser. I took kissing very seriously, and I still do. I've always thought of kissing as an art form so I practiced almost daily with a Chico stick candy bar at home. I made sure I knew how to circle my tongue perfectly. I was really good at it because as you know Chico sticks are grainy and rough like sand paper, one wrong move and I would scrape my tongue. I guess that gentleness helped me out because when I kissed boys they were amazed at how I could maneuver and coordinate so perfectly. What they didn't know was I was happy that their tongues couldn't cut me. I enjoyed kissing so much my average kiss lasted about 15 to 20 minutes before I'd stop. I was a fast little 8th grader!

"A Piece of Peace"

The past can propel you to purpose but does not dictate it.

My environment couldn't erase my ending. God purposed my being born in the projects of Chicago. He knew who my parents would be and what challenges I'd experience long before I arrived. He was tilling the ground for greatness. I learned survival skills on the streets and the art of effective persuasion by taking a stand for what I believed in.

We are not called to our past nor bound by it. It does not determine our destiny. It is at best a reminder of how far we've come and how much we've overcome. When we look forward instead of backwards we are able to see what's coming. It's when we live our life in the rear view mirror of our mind that we get lost on the current journey and could even end up wrecking our lives. **God doesn't dwell in our past. He's *patient* with our present, *proud* of our progress and *focused* on our future.** The seeds that were planted in your childhood can be dug up and you can plant seeds that are more nutritious and therefore, more productive.

Take a look at the past of these men and women of the Bible to be reminded of God's view:
Jesus went from a stable to our Savior.
David the adulterer and liar was an anointed leader.
Joseph was sold as a slave but promoted to a supplier.
Ruth went from widower to the wonderful lineage of Jesus.
Rahab went from prostitute to protector to princess.
Saul was a persecutor who later proclaimed the Gospel.

Another name for **PURPOSE** is **PRODUCTIVITY**. Be productive now! Being **PRODUCTIVE** means being fruitful, useful, creative and industrious. Do not diminish your destiny due to a slow, small or seemingly insignificant start. No matter how bad or bleak the past looks your future can be adjusted instantly if you **focus on God's forecast.**

A poem

"Hidden Son-Shine"

How can something beautiful shine thru a cold gray haze?
Every obstacle was used to establish endurance
Blunt blows to my heart, forced it to beat stronger and faster
Each salt tear I cried cleansed my soul
Challenges created coping muscles
Disappointments delivered me from impatience
Violation pushed me to victory through empowerment
Persistence became the pavement for my purpose
I never quit
I remembered where I came from
I always look forward

When I couldn't visibly see financial freedom
    I stretched the checkbook of my mind
    Balanced my ideas and my time
    Calculated fear and limitation
        as having no value or worth in my situation
The sum total of my reality is,
    I can't be stressed
Cause God's view of me is BEYOND BLESSED!

Chapter 2

Shhh, Don't Tell Nobody

What the devil meant for bad…God worked out for good.

After I graduated elementary school I ended up going back to Altgeld Gardens for High School. Chicago held lottery drawings for school selections in my neighborhood. I didn't win an opportunity to go to the new schools (Corliss & Julian) that were close to where I lived so I decided to go back to what was familiar. Things were a lot different as a teenager in the projects. I grew up real fast and lost something real precious…my innocence.

By the time I started Carver High School I had traded in the cigarettes for marijuana. I never allowed the pot to keep me from class or my activities. As a matter of fact my teachers never even knew I smoked it. I was involved in almost every activity in High School. I was co-captain and a starter on the basketball team, captain of the pom-pom squad, member of the track team, dance troop, and girl's chorus. I was voted the most popular girl in my high school and I won Prom Queen. As for academics, I was the secretary of the Future Business Leaders of America and an honor roll student. And all this was done while occasionally smoking pot. However the odor of marijuana took a back seat to the putrid stench I inhaled daily at my high school. Carver was built on top of a landfill and the smell of hot old garbage ruled the atmosphere. I guess the logic was to build a school on garbage because nothing but trash would attend.

As a teenager in Altgeld I could always count on fireworks and candy. I'm not speaking of the firecrackers or sparkles to celebrate the 4th of July or the tasty nut chews, lemon heads, Boston baked beans, blow pops and slow pokes you could purchase from the penny candy lady or the local grocery store. The fireworks I'm referring to were white lightning flashes from the barrel of a gun you'd see as you ran inside and ducked to avoid a stray bullet from the occasional drive by shootings. The candy I'm talking about was the drug dealers kind, "make me feel good" sweets they pushed in the hood simply because the reality of the situation appeared hopeless and drugs made people forget about their responsibility.

You see in our community we would get high and transport ourselves to wonderful places, like the land of 'OZ'…On Zoom. No bills, no creditors, no fussing and fighting were allowed there…just the munchies, real deep incomprehensible conversation, and laughter at corny jokes. It's what we would call 'good times'. The only problem with getting drunk or smoking marijuana was it messed with and messed up your mind. After you'd come down from the unrealistic high you still had to deal with reality. Your mind may have been transported to Fantasy Island but your situation and your responsibility remained the same or took a turn for the worse. The good news was I never did hard drugs or pills. My drug of choice was weed.

As a freshman in high school, I started experimenting with dating. Momma was still working the evening shift so I would sneak and have company over after school. One day my boyfriend Alex came by and my dad called to check up on my sister and me. I made the mistake of laughing when I picked up the phone. He suspiciously started drilling me with questions and the next thing I knew he had hung up on me and was headed my way.

I tried to play it cool by mentioning to Alex he should head home so he could be rested for basketball practice the next day, but he wasn't trying to hear me. Alex was a junior in high school, 6 foot 7 inches tall, a starter on the basketball team, and to top it all off he was a dark chocolate mocha mousse masterpiece! You don't get rid of boys like him - you do what you can to keep them around. After about 20 minutes of talking and kissing the doorbell rang. I told Alex I thought it was my dad and that he needed to leave out the back door because my dad was kind of crazy.

At the same time, my dad had begun to make his way to the back of the house. Just as Alex closed the screen my dad (who was about 2 feet from him) reached out to grab him. Thank God my dad didn't have his gun. He always carried a gun in the glove compartment of his car. Alex took off running towards the fence with my dad chasing close behind. Just as Alex began climbing, my dad grabbed his foot and caused him to get tangled in the fence. He twisted his ankle, but eventually managed to escape to the nearest bus stop.

He ended up on the injured list for 3 games because of his sprained ankle, and I ended up with the beating of my life. My dad ripped another hole in my butt. In our house my parents lived by the scripture "spare the rod spoil the child"…in other words they believed in whippings. That day my dad whipped my butt with his big black leather belt so hard I think I had welts on my legs and behind for 2 weeks afterward. As he painstakingly verbally chastised me, his breath reeked of Jack Daniels whiskey. While lowering the leather to my legs and butt each stroke was accompanied by a syllable of a word. He exclaimed *"did-n't-I-tell-you-not-to-have-com-pa-ny-while-no-bo-dy-was-home?"* He continued until he got tired. It felt like hours but it was probably only about 10 minutes.

I was lucky he didn't kill me since I knew I wasn't suppose to have company while momma was at work, let alone *boy* company. Shortly after that incident I started staying the night over my moms best friend Lenora's house in Altgeld gardens with my "play cousin" Brenda on the weekends. Momma didn't mind because my older sister only had to watch one of us while she was at work. Moms just wanted an adult to keep an eye on me. What my mom didn't know was there were no rules or curfew laws at Brenda's house. So we could pretty much do whatever we wanted to as long as it was outside of the house.

Our favorite pastime was to get drunk and smoke pot together. By this time I was smoking more regularly and my drink of choice was wild Irish rose wine or mad dog 20/20. One night while hanging out with Brenda at her boyfriend's house, we had been smoking and drinking more than usual. We were so high we decided to sleep over her boyfriend's house on the couch. At the time, we were virgins and were planning on keeping it that way. At around one o'clock in the morning I heard some noise and I glanced up from my end of the sofa and Brenda was heading into her boyfriends Charles' room. I was too buzzed to stop her so I went back to sleep.

All of a sudden I was being lifted off the couch and carried into a room and forcefully thrown onto a twin bed. By the time I realized what was going on it was too late. There were 5 grown men standing over me and holding my legs and arms down. My cousin's boyfriend Charles was sitting next to the bed with his head in his hands. I pleaded with him not to let this happen as one of the guys put his hands over my mouth to drown out my screams. Another guy took my pants and panties off. Just then one of the guys yelled out *"damn she's on her period man"* and another voice said *"good then we ain't got to worry about her getting pregnant."*

Then they each took turns raping me repeatedly. I struggled to break free but I must have blacked out during the tussle from exhaustion. When I woke up I barely remembered the incident. I felt like something had happened, but I didn't have any proof.

While walking home with my cousin I hesitantly told her what I thought had happened, not sure if it was a nightmare or if I was still trippin' off the drugs. When we got to her place I immediately headed to the bathroom. I knew what time of the month it was. I had been searching my mind for clues from the men violating me. I knew what I was looking for would become the only piece of proof I'd have for what actually took place that night.

My worst fear became a reality. I just sat there on the toilet. Numb. Silent. Violated. Afraid. After all, because I had been smoking marijuana and drinking alcohol, who would believe me? It would have been my word against theirs. My dad would have killed me if he knew what happened. My mom had enough on her plate putting my brother through medical school while raising the rest of us.

So I stayed silent, and I never reported the incident. My cousin broke up with her boyfriend Charles and I never saw him or those other men again in my life. I also decided I wouldn't tell anybody else about what happened. On the outside I carried on a normal life, but inside I had become grown before my time.

"A Piece of Peace"

What the devil meant for bad…God worked out for good.

I walked away from that incident alive. Although I was emotionally scarred, my life was spared. I didn't have to carry the burden of a rapist' baby inside my belly, I was disease free, and amazingly it didn't affect my schoolwork or personal relationships with friends and peers.

Physical violation affects people in different ways, for me it became an internal crutch. I processed promiscuity as a byproduct of having been raped. I leaned on it as a source of security when I felt insecure. I believed if I offered myself no one would ever have the power to take advantage of me again. I didn't realize I was attempting to cover up the permanent scar I saw in my mind. It took years for me to erase the error I had accidentally etched in stone. I am grateful the image finally got deleted off my 'heart drive.'

I believe God enables people to go through rough situations to be a reminder of His strength. **If you've been raped, molested, or have endured any other form of physical violation it was not your fault!** And no matter what you were wearing or doing at the time, it will never be considered your fault.

If you kept it a secret at the time, it was the best choice for that hour. If you shared it and no one believed you please understand that people sometimes don't accept or can't handle the truth. Either they didn't believe it or they already knew it and felt guilty for not doing something about it. Sometimes people even feel helpless for not being in a position to prevent it.

If you feel hatred in your heart towards your offender(s), you must learn to forgive them or you are still allowing them to violate you now. People do not automatically have power over us - we have to give them control. We give it to them by not allowing forgiveness in our heart, which is how we heal.

God forgives us daily. How can we ask God for forgiveness, expect and know we will receive it if we ourselves, harbor **unforgiveness** or ill will against our enemies or people who have wronged us? When we do that we become hypocrites. We don't have to wear negative labels, God gives us the ability to trade hate and **unforgiveness** in and replace them with love. Since God is our dad and He is love we should look like His children and reflect His goodness, not our personal weaknesses.

The beauty-FULL thing about forgiveness is it reflects His love and grace, which enables our mental load to be much lighter. If our mind is at ease, we are positioned under His spout so that He can fill us up in order to pour into the lives of others.

Don't allow the face of **UNFORGIVNESS** to **DISTRACT** you from your destiny.

A poem

"ESB not ESP"

I Play peek-a-boo with the Sun light
Embrace dark days and rainy nights
See thru tough storms and trying times
Believe despair and defeat are a state of mind

I **E**MBRACE, **S**EE and **B**ELIEVE
Whatever I strive for, I always achieve
I am no better than you
Only your eyes can choose your view

The back of tapestry is always tangled
Why look at the rear when you can change your angle
If you are facing forward and looking up
You're in position for God to fill your cup
You'll be so full others can sip from your saucer
There will be enough for your sons and daughters
When you are in place under His spout
He will tailor make a blessing to work things out

Just make sure your life is lined up with the Word
You'll have fewer challenges and a lot less strife
So give it your all and try your very best
With the right undercurrent you'll reach greatness
If you **embrace**, **see** and **believe**
What ever you strive for, you'll have to achieve

Chapter 3

Fun Town Bad State

Out of His will…spinning on a wheel.

At 15 I was dating an 18-year-old fine Creole boy named RJ. Kickin' it with an older boy was pretty special to me, since in my early teen years I was called 'itty-bitty titty committee' and ironing board due to my lack of curves. We were spending a lot of time together hanging out at clubs, listening to music, smoking weed, and having sex. We were having sex a lot. Since I was no longer a virgin he became my first love, or shall I say lust.

I wasn't on any form of birth control so RJ assured me he was "pulling out" before ejaculating. Well needless to say his pull out method was off. I got pregnant. I was terrified of being pregnant. I was a junior in high school and I knew that if my mother found out she would kill me. I told my oldest sister Erma that I was pregnant and wanted an abortion, and she in turn sold me out at the dinner table.

We were eating some brown sugar fried chicken wings that moms was famous for making, when my sister mid bite says *"ma guess who's pregnant?"* I was stunned and afraid. I closed my eyes and braced myself for a stiff slap across the face since I was sitting right next to my mother when my sister told on me. But my mom having raised 4 girls simply said *"I knew that was gon' happen sooner or later. You and Reggie have been spending a lot of time together. So what you gonna do?"*

I sat there crying, shocked and livid at Erma for telling her. When I was finally able to speak I mumbled, *"I want an abortion"*. My mother said calmly *"That's your decision. Let it be on your hands not mine if you can't have kids later in life."* Honestly being concerned about kids later in life was the furthest thing from my mind. I was worried about finishing high school and going to college, not to mention enjoying being a teenager before I was a mother.

I searched through the phone book looking for a place to get it done. I made an appointment at Planned Parenthood on 87th and State. I had been working since I was about 12 years old and I had saved nearly every cent I had made. I had the $250.00 it cost to get the abortion but I was under age so I needed my mother's signature to take money out of my savings account. My mother took me to the bank and got the money out and the next day Erma drove me to the clinic. I was ok until I got there and saw young girls with their boyfriends. I really wanted RJ to come with me, but when I told him that I wasn't going to keep the baby he was so upset he moved back to Louisiana to live with his father. It was years later before I saw him again.

I sat in the waiting area for what seemed like hours until finally they called my name. They gave me a gown and told me to dress with the opening in the front and to wait in the small room in the back on the right. The room was cold, stoic and white. It seemed so sterile and bland...no pictures, no mirror, just a propped up bed on wheels. The bed was in the center of the room and beside it was a covered table on wheels. There was a strong scent seeping from the small space causing me to almost taste the medicine in the air. The piercing sounds of little girls screaming, crying and whaling instantly ignited my fear. I tried to focus on the fact that it was the best thing for me to do since I was still in high school and I really wanted to go to college.

Just when my mind started to wander to "what if," the doctor walked in along with a nurse. The nurse uncovered what must have been 20 different pieces of metal hardware they were probably going to use on me during the procedure. I inhaled and tried not to look at the size or shapes of the instruments, but it was impossible not to.

I tried to relax and stay calm as the doctor had me place my feet into the metal stirrups. When he placed his cold hand covered with a plastic glove on my abdomen I quickly contracted. He calmly said *"Relax. I've got to put some jelly inside you. It'll feel rather cold. Then you're going to feel some pressure and a slight pulling sensation inside."* I nodded as he reached for one of the big metal tools from the table. I tensed up so tightly he had to ask me to relax again.

I got dizzy from partially holding my breath because I was so scared. The nurse told me to breath…I began to inhale and exhale deeply while looking up at the white ceiling as the nurse gently reached for my hand. I remember a loud sound, kind of like a vacuum cleaner and then I felt a pulling, a gnawing, and an extremely painful tugging from the inside of me. I cried and screamed out in agony but to no avail. He continued to suck out the life that had begun to form inside me.

I immediately dreaded the disgusting deed that would haunt me and leave me physically dirty and mentally damaged for years to come. There was blood on the sheets, my gown everywhere…so much blood, and so much noise and so much pain and so little left of the life that was now in a trashcan conveniently placed beside the bed. I had just rid myself of a mini me. My carelessness ceased the creation of God's gift to have a chance to be all it was conceived to be, because I pulled the plug of possibility.

After the process was complete, the nurse gave me the longest sanitary napkin I had ever seen in my life, it reached from my navel to the small of my back. She told me to put it on, gave me a clean gown and said she'd be back in a few minutes. She returned and helped me walk to the recovery area where other young girls laid in tears and excruciating pain, each of us contemplating our decision to eradicate our unborn child. We were young but no longer were innocent. The guilt and blood of our unborn babies would forever stain our hands and hearts, and one day we would all have to answer for our actions.

After about 1 ½ hours in the recovery area the nurse brought me some release papers to sign and a prescription to pickup my medicine. Then she called for my sister to escort me home. As we drove home there was deadening silence in the car. Neither one of us were able to articulate the enormity of my action. I vaguely remember my sister stopping at the drug store to pick up my painkillers and antibiotics. Before long we were pulling up in front of the house. When we walked in momma was a nervous wreck, pacing and wringing her hands. I'd never seen her look so worried. Too overwhelmed with my own pain to question her, I headed into my room to lie down.

My mom walked in shortly afterwards and began to share with me news that pierced me right in the center of my abdomen. It was more pointed and painful than the scraping and vacuuming I had already endured at Planned Parenthood previously. She cautiously shared with me her concerns about my having to use my hard earned summer job money to get the abortion. She expressed her desire to help me. Slowly she lowered the guillotine.

"I called your father. (pause) I asked him for some money".

At this point, my mom is visibly looking terrified.

"I didn't know he was going to get that upset and react the way he did. I told him that you had gotten pregnant and needed…"(pause)

"Momma. No. Momma no! How could you? Why would you do that"?

I am literally screaming and crying so hard my head is about to explode, immediately I get a migraine. She continues…

"After I told him we needed the money so you could get an abortion he started cursing me out and threatening to kill us. I didn't know what to do so I told him it wasn't true, that I made it up to get some money from him to help me with my bills and mortgage this month. He didn't believe me. He's on his way over to pick you and Dale (my little sister) up to take you to Fun Town".

Fun Town is an amusement park on 95th in Stony Island Avenue that my sister and I loved to go to. It has roller coasters, bumper cars and merry-go-rounds. We usually ride nearly all the rides, eat junk food and play games. It's like a mini Great America, Six Flags, or Magic Mountain. There was no way in the world I could go there while being in excruciating pain. I was devastated and petrified at just the thought of it. But one thing I knew…I was daddy's girl and if he found out I had an abortion he'd kill RJ and me. My very first real acting job was about to take place.

I took some extra painkillers and washed my face and tried to mentally prepare for the role I was about to perform. My dad got there and my sister and me were all smiles and I was acting excited about going. As I hugged him I smelled the stench of the hava tampa cigars he smoked lodged in his skin and shirt. His eyes were blood shot darting back and forth between my mother and me. He was carefully checking us out. My mom remained calm and I was extra enthusiastic.

The three of us headed towards his green and white Buick Century. My little sister Dale knew I was in pain so she immediately yelled out…*'I got the front seat coming and going"*. Just like most kids we had to verbally claim the front seat. This day was no different, she knew there was no way I could sit next to my dad without him seeing me wince and cringe in pain as the clots of blood passed through my frail young body. I was relieved she called the front seat. My pain came in waves, and was persistent, sharp and without warning. It was so frequent and blunt that it would catch me totally off guard. The pain… I imagine, only compares to what an expecting mother feels while having contractions prior to delivery. Unbelievable and indescribable!

When we arrived at Fun Town my sister and I headed for the ferris wheel. Once on board I began to cry as my little sister comforted me and rubbed my hand. I only had a small window to give into my pain because by the time the wheel reached near the bottom I had to show my pearly whites. My dad stood there watching us go round and round while smoking his big brown cigar. His hands were big and strong and he had thick dark colored nails that he kept neatly trimmed. My dads commanding hands also served as a reminder that he was DAD, MAN, STRONG and POWERFUL. I spent the day "acting" happy and cheerful and my father never knew I felt like I was on my deathbed. It would be years later before I would learn to forgive my mom for involving my dad, not to mention forgiving myself for emptying my womb.

"A Piece of Peace"

Out of His will…spinning on a wheel.

I made grown up decisions, participated in grown folk behavior and almost became a mother before I learned how to be a child. I attempted to blame my sexual behavior on the rape incident that had taken place previously and it was years later before I realized that my past didn't have the power to pollute my present. I had to be responsible for my actions and own up to them. When I decided to have sex at the age of 15 I knew exactly what I was doing. I knew the possible outcome yet I went forward with the act.

I don't know about you but when things go wrong in my life, I'm usually the first to beat myself up. I put myself inside the boxing ring and I don't need friends or family to take punches at me because I can hit myself harder than anyone else. I had to learn how to forgive me. I didn't think I was worthy of forgiveness. I certainly didn't think God could forgive me. However, that would have meant the sacrifice Christ made on the cross for my sins was in vain. I knew that was a lie, a trick straight from the enemy (or inner me which can be one in the same). We must learn how to own our errors without replaying our wrongs. We cannot carry the **GUILT** by hitting the repeat button in our mind. You can drive yourself crazy doing that.

I would also place other people in the ring with me because I didn't want to carry the burden of a bad decision alone. My not being forgiving towards my mother was interesting because I was the one who did the deed she was just trying to help. The outcome of her action was not her original intention. How many times have we blamed others for our mistakes? **For if ye forgive men their trespasses, your heavenly Father will also forgive you: But if ye forgive not men their trespasses, neither will your Father forgive your trespasses. Matthew 6:14-15**

An ugly face of distraction is "**GUILT**." When we ask God for forgiveness with a sincere heart He cast our sins as far away as the East is from the West. We are the ones who hold sins so close it separates us from our Savior.

Recognize the **FACE** of the culprit trying to **DISTRACT** you from reaching your full potential. Put **GUILT** in the garbage along with the rest of the trash.

Chapter 4

My Exodus²

Speak Lord…your servant is listening.

While growing up moms made it perfectly clear she couldn't afford to send me to college. I took typing classes to ensure I had a trade to offer corporate America. I was typing 70 words per minute by the time I finished my high school typing classes. My mom had pretty much depleted what financial resources she had, putting one of my older brothers through medical school. Not to mention that my two older sisters had made her a grandmother at an early age. One sister got pregnant right after high school and the other got pregnant in her sophomore year of college and had to drop out.

I think moms feared I would follow in their footsteps so she decided to keep me close to home. But I was and have always been an adventurer. I knew I would one day go to college and have the opportunity to make lemonade out of the lemons sitting stagnant in my fruit bowl.

I had a terrible memory as a result of my smoking marijuana so I developed a great way to retain information. This idea actually helped pave the way to my profession. I use to read history lessons and turn them into rap songs to remember them. My memory only worked if the information I had to recall had a beat or a rhyme. I became really good at making up rhymes off the top of my head and putting historic information into rap songs.

One day while taking a major exam in history I was caught bopping my head and mumbling under my breath. My high school history teacher Ms. Brown questioned me directly following the test. I shared with her that I had "memorized" the entire lesson and put it into a rap song. She didn't understand so I demonstrated it for her in front of the whole class. It was personally one of the most amazing, energizing, and memorable moments I had ever experienced. For the first time in my life I actually had an ability to hit a switch to make the light bulb shine in other peoples minds. The students were responding to my rhymes. The answers were flowing from my lips and as they heard me they responded verbally.

I had created a legitimate way to disseminate information about history and at the same time it became fun to learn. Some students cheered because the rhymes were a confirmation to a question they'd answered correctly. Other students sighed in frustration as my rhymes revealed wrong answers to their test questions. When I finished flowing and rapping Ms. Brown was pleasantly surprised at the fact that I actually knew my history and had the correct information stored in a format that made sense to not only me but the class as well. She was so impressed she spoke with Mr. Harris, a teacher in the music department.

Mr. Harris was an extremely forward thinking man. He was aware that rap music was on the verge of becoming the next big thing. Legendary rappers like The Sugar Hill Gang and Curtis Blow had hit the radio scene strong, so Mr. Harris created a concept to raise money for our senior yearbook and prom activities. He decided to do an album as a fundraiser. It would be the first time a high school had ever produced an album, let alone an inner city school.

I was selected to be a lead rapper along side deep voiced Barry," Orlando better know as "O", Jess Bone and several others. We spent long nights in a studio perfecting our lyrics and rhymes. Our parents consented to the project and we sacrificed sleep and worked extra hard on our homework to make sure we were good examples of what we were rapping about. Our project was about being cool and the need to stay in school.

Our hard work paid off. We made history! We received worldwide recognition for completing the positive and educational album we titled "Get Live 83". We were instant local celebrities, signing autographs, making appearances at record stores and being interviewed by news anchors and newspaper reporters. The bug of the entertainment industry bit me that year!

I stopped smoking marijuana by the time we started working on the album. I was channeling all that restless energy into something constructive. Shortly after the success of our high school album another miracle crossed my path. There was a national search for a 'stay in school project' with none other than the "King of Rap" himself Curtis Blow. Mr. Harris entered Barry and I in the contest and we won! Barry and I recorded a rap song with Curtis Blow and got paid quite a bit of money for doing it!

God is a restorer and a redeemer. He who began a good work in you is faithful to complete it. The gray haze from growing up in the ghetto was now becoming a pretty pink! Life was getting good. I've always been a firm believer in saving money. Thank God I saved the money from summer jobs and the album because after I graduated high school my mom reiterated there was no money for me to get a higher education. But the voice inside my heart spoke louder. **God had a ram in the bush or shall I say the bank!**

I believed I would go to college one day. I also knew it would take some major convincing for my mother to understand how. I began to prepare for what I desired by researching and filling out college applications. I was accepted by my first choice, Southern Illinois University in Carbondale (SIU-C). I couldn't tell moms until I had all my ducks in a row. I had money saved and I was admitted but I still had to prove to my mother that I wouldn't need her financial help while away from home.

The summer before school started I worked and saved my paychecks. I only used my earnings to purchase items I needed for dorm life on campus. Since moms still worked the evening shift I was able to easily plot and plan my 1st exodus. My mother wasn't nosey and she never went into my room when I wasn't home. She had a rule, keep your door closed if your room was a mess. I kept my door closed, not because my room wasn't neat but because I was hiding a big black and silver footlocker chest along with the supplies I needed for college inside.

As the fall semester drew near I still hadn't figured out how I was going to break the news to her. Most parents would have been pleased that their child applied for school, registered and could afford to go to college without their help. However my mom would require some assistance with understanding that simple truth.

It was one week prior to school starting and I still hadn't figured out a way to break the news to my mom. I also hadn't figured out how I was going to get my things to Carbondale, Illinois, which was about a 6-hour drive from us. I had a possible back up plan to take the Greyhound bus and ship my belongings since Greyhound did frequent trips to SIU-C for a reasonable price, but shipping my things separately concerned me.

The day I got caught off guard I had just finished eating. I went into my room and I didn't know my mom was right behind me. She opened up my door to tell me to wash the dishes and discovered the huge metal footlocker sitting smack dab in the middle of my bedroom floor. I looked up speechless like a little girl caught with her hand in the cookie jar.

She asked about the footlocker and I explained to her I was going away to college and that she didn't have anything to worry about, it was all taken care of. She asked about admissions, financial aid and school fees. I settled her concerns by fibbing a little. I told my mom the tuition was totally paid off for the full 4 years when actually my savings only covered one year of tuition, supplies and housing. I received grants, took out a loan and worked every year I was in college. I had always been financially responsible and I wasn't a stranger to working so I knew I would do whatever needed to be done to repay the loan without penalty. My mother believed me, and when my father heard about my plans he quickly volunteered to rent a van to drive my belongings and me to Carbondale.

Once I settled into school at SIU-C, I rarely went home, and unlike most students I never got home sick. I have to thank my dad for that. He began in the fall of 1983 a weekly tradition that is still in effect even to this day. He started calling me early Sunday morning to hear my voice, see if I needed anything, and to let me know how everyone was. Every week I looked forward to his 5-minute conversation. It also relieved some anxiety I had built up about not having a father around constantly while growing up. The truth of the matter is, a dad is needed at any stage of your life. The fact that my dad was there for me at an age where I could comprehend his support, love and concern for me, meant the world to me and I am better as a result of having experienced it.

I was extremely active in college. After all, SIU-C was famous for being a party school. It was known for the "Kappa carnival" (a week long Black Greek event) way back in the day, and was home of the "Salukis," a winning football team. I was involved in all sorts of activities from scholastic to social and everything in between.

My natural high came from being on stage. My introduction to theatre could be considered an accident. A friend of mine name Bill Kincaid a big fan of my singing invited me to audition for "Little Shop of Horror," a stage play at McCloud theatre. Acting was foreign to me. I had never taken an acting class or acted in anything, outside of my "Fun Town fright night" experience, but since it was a musical and they needed some black singers I took him up on his offer and auditioned.

Acting was like breathing for me. The director, George Penny, took notice of my level of confidence in this foreign arena. He was so pleased with my natural ability at the audition that he cast me in the play and invited me to his invitation only acting class. Although acting was challenging,

I was the most comfortable I had ever been in my life. Walking onto stage was as easy to me as opening a door and going inside.

In addition to studying in the theatre department, I worked on "Day Break" a TV news program on campus as a producer and camera operator. My love for speaking would pay off, as I became a radio personality for WIDB, a local campus radio station. I worked the overnight shift and did a quiet storm program full of oldies but goodies like the ones I heard the wine-o's singing on the street corner growing up in Altgeld.

Since I've always believed in leading a balanced life, as I was watering academic seeds I planted some seeds of personal pleasure. I got involved in some social and service groups on campus. I really liked dancing so I auditioned for the hottest dance group in the Midwest. I joined the Black Fire Dancers (BFD) a popular dance squad on campus. We performed tight choreographed routines at school func-tions, fundraisers, and correctional institutions. One of our most requested performances was "Thriller" by Michael Jackson. We performed it complete with bloody make up, raggedy costumes and the infamous pelvic gyrations that were seen in the actual "Thriller" music videos.

SIU-C was a predominately white institution but the black Greek organizations were in full force. All of the fraternities and sororities were well represented. On campus we had the brothers of Alpha Phi Alpha, Omega Psi Phi, Phi Beta Sigma, Kappa Alpha Psi, Iota Phi Theta, and the sisters of Alpha Kappa Alpha, Delta Sigma Theta, Zeta Phi Beta and Sigma Gamma Rho. Although my favorite color pink was the official hue of Alpha Kappa Alpha, I had an instant rapport with the ladies of Delta Sigma Theta (DST).

Pledging DST was difficult, however, when I accepted the first assignment there was no way I could turn back. I had already begun a series that was summoning me to the finish line. We pledged for 8 weeks straight, before we completed the pledge process and crossed the burning sands.

Singing was my thing so I joined the SIU-C jazz ensemble and toured in and out of town singing and scatting. Anita Baker was the hot voice at the time and I would cover her most popular songs. I had 2 challenges, the first was singing lead with a live band, the second was trying to decipher what the heck Anita was singing. She has a great sound but most of the time no one had any idea what she was singing. But I loved that woman's voice!

I was involved in the school of communication, the school of drama and the school of music and arts in college so I had a tough time deciding which one I wanted to major in. I got an idea stuck in my head about creating my own major in order to combine everything I loved. I met with the dean of communications and explained what I wanted to do and he requested a written proposal detailing my scholastic plan. I submitted a proposal for the major I created called "theatrical broadcasting," and it was accepted as a valid attainable major.

In the spring of 1988 I graduated with a BA degree in "theatrical broadcasting." It combined radio, television, theatre, dance and music. I had no idea that it was a sanctified set up. It laid the foundation for exposure to all forms of media and arts. I had experience in front of and behind the camera producing, and as an on-air radio personality. It allowed me the opportunity to develop my stage presence while singing and acting for audiences. It presented variety and the basis for my becoming a trailblazer. I didn't fit inside anyone's pre-sized box because the design for my destiny had yet to be discovered. I was journeying in a direction full of hope and possibilities so that I could make a living doing what I love to do.

Upon completion of college I went back to Chicago and got a job selling air, on-air advertisements for radio stations that is. As a telemarketing sales person for a major station, I not only capitalized on my power of persuasion but I also discovered that my voice was trained to be an asset in the advertising industry. I exceeded all of the set quotas and was promoted to a commission only status within a month of being employed. I sold radio time for approximately 3 months. Then one day I woke up believing I should work for Ted Turner. At the time I hadn't done any research on Ted Turner or his company. There were students at SIU-C who spoke about applying for a VJ (Video Journalist) position at CNN. I heard the salary was only $15,000 per year and to me that salary sounded like they would be partially paid interns. It didn't interest me until I heard the 'Ted Turner" clock ticking louder than the sound of my own heartbeat. I was obedient and followed its lead.

I spoke with the telemarketing supervisor at work that Monday and requested a week off. My request was denied because I had only worked for the company a few months. What I knew to be true on the inside was so much more than the current security I had, after all it was just a job. I wanted a career. I quit and management assured me I would be re-hired if I ever needed a job since I was one of their top sales producers.

I went home that evening and plotted out a plan. I woke up Tuesday morning, went to the store to get the Sun-times newspaper and began my search for a rental car. My mom saw me looking through the newspaper and heard me making calls inquiring about rentals so she asked if I wanted to use her car. This wasn't unusual for my mom; she was very generous when it came to her vehicle. If I needed to use her car all day she'd let me take her to work and pick her up at 11pm. This time I had a different agenda so I said very confidently

"Thanks Ma, but I'm renting a car to go to Atlanta. I'm gonna work for Ted".

"Ted who"? She replied.

"Ted Turner, the owner of CNN, Turner Broadcasting Systems and TNT in Atlanta, Georgia.

"Oh, you have an interview with him?" she inquired.

"No, I haven't sent him my resume but I feel like I am supposed to work for him. So I'm going there to find out how I can get a job somewhere in his company."

At this point she could clearly see I was serious. One thing my mom has never questioned was my determination or tenacity, mainly because I inherited it from her. She has always set goals and accomplished them so I just followed in her footsteps.

"Well, I told you I'd help you get a car when you graduated" she stated.

This had become my mother's tradition over the years. When each one of us graduated she would put the down payment on a car as a graduation gift. My mother spouted out in a loud and authoritative voice *"gone and get dressed so we can get you a car and get back by noon so I won't be late for work."* She didn't even stop to think about how much money she needed. She was a planner who was always financially prepared for rainy days. I quickly exited the kitchen table and got dressed. I didn't even shower that morning for fear that she might change her mind if I took too long. Besides when momma said to do something, she usually meant she wanted it done yesterday.

We drove to the Nissan dealer on 159th street in River Oaks about 10 miles from our house. We looked at a few cars and then saw a new black Nissan Sentra that we thought was a fair price. I test-drove it and liked it. Even though I had excellent credit, when we sat down to do the paper work with the dealer a small monkey wrench got thrown in the program. The dealer asked my mom to co-sign on the loan since I had quit my job and was technically unemployed.

My mother gave me 'the look' and then tilted her head forcefully and quickly towards the door a few times, gesturing for me to step outside the man's tiny 4x4 office.

"We'll be right back," she said to the dealer. With tight lips and a low voice she put my little butt in check, asking me why I was wasting her time and putting her on the spot.

"I thought you said you had good credit"

"I do. I have perfect credit".

"Then why is he asking me to co-sign for your car? I'm not going to be responsible for your bills. I've got my own bills to pay. I don't have time to drive all the way down here trying to help you out only to have to head back home without a car".

"Ma, I have over $5,000 saved up right now. And my boss said I could come back to work if Atlanta doesn't work out for me. I promise you, you will not have to pay one single note on my car. Ma remember, I'm the one who went to college without you ever having to pay one cent for tuition, housing or my apartment...I promise I'll pay my note every month on time".

She acquiesced. We signed the papers and I drove my brand new 1988 black 2-door Nissan Sentra home and packed for my journey to Atlanta. I didn't know where I was going to stay nor did I have friends or relatives who resided in Atlanta, all I had was the address and phone number to TBS, a map and an internal nudging that pulled me beyond my sight. **Hebrews 11:1 Faith is the substance of things hoped for the evidence of things unseen. My 2ⁿᵈ Exodus**

I secured a room at a hotel downtown about 5 minutes from the CNN building. I called the TBS human resource department and was instructed to pick up an application and leave it with the security desk on the first floor. I hung up and prepared for my destiny. I put on a business suit and collected my briefcase loaded with resume, photos, and references from college. I arrived at the beautiful edifice and marveled at its size and structure. I asked the guard at the security desk for an application for TBS and proceeded down the long escalator to the lower level courtyard.

I read the application then pulled out my typed information with dates of previous jobs, former addresses and important phone numbers. I was extremely careful to avoid mistakes and scratch outs on the application. Once I was done I went back up the moving stairs and requested a line to the human resource department. A woman name Susan answered sounding very busy. I informed her I'd completed my application and wanted to personally bring it up.

"Just leave it with the security desk" she stated in a short routine way.

"I would love for you to put a face with the paper work, as I am a graduate of Southern Illinois University and I have worked for WSIU-TV and WIDB radio and I am only in Atlanta for a couple of days." I stated very confidently yet with a hopeful heart. Well as God would have it, favor was before me, she was hesitant but requested to speak to the security guard who proceeded to give me directions to her office.

"Thank you." I said almost sing songy. I was excited but I managed to remain cool and calm on the outside. I walked into her office and she shook my hand and then reached for my application, quickly glancing at my experience and skills.

"You type 70 words per minute?"

"Yes", I replied.

"Good. We're always looking for strong typists."

"I see the only experience you have in broadcasting is your work with your schools TV station. She continued. *Our VJ positions fill up almost a year in advance but I'll keep your resume on file in case someone doesn't work out. The address on this resume is in Chicago, do you live here or there?"*

"I live in Chicago, but I'm willing to relocate." I said very quickly and decisively. She placed the application on her desk and looked me dead in the eyes for the first time and said

"I'm going to tell you the truth. If a temporary position opens up it usually needs filling within a few days. I won't have time to wait for someone to come from Chicago. I'm sorry I need someone local."

Just then the phone rang almost on cue, she answered it waved and mouthed thank you and goodbye. I smiled, mouthed thank you and exited. I was standing at the elevator waiting to ride it down to the level of my now lowered enthusiasm when I heard Susan calling my name. *"Maura, Maura, one of the assistants on Ted Turners floor went on a 3-month leave of absence and they are in need of someone ASAP. You fit the qualifications. Would you be interested in a 3 month temporary assignment?"*

"Yes, of course." This was an answered prayer.

She asked me to accompany her to the 14th floor to meet Debbie Monger the executive assistant to Robert Wussler a corporate VP. Debbie was the supervisor of the position. She wanted someone who dressed corporate, had good typing skills and could answer the phones. I met Debbie. We hit it off instantly and I was offered the job.

Susan and I headed back to her office and completed the paper work, and I was given the start date of August 8, 1988, translation 8-8-88. Biblically the number 7 represents completion and since God is a beginning and an ending God, the number 8 must mean new beginnings! This was definitely a new beginning. I called my family and told them I was driving back in the morning and I would be relocating to Atlanta Georgia over the weekend.

I searched for an apartment the rest of the day and filled out a few applications. I checked out of my hotel the next morning and drove the 7 hours back to Chicago. I loaded my car with as many clothes as I could carry, withdrew some cash, and requested a cashier's check for the balance of my account. I drove back to Atlanta Saturday morning and on Sunday morning I found an apartment. I just had to wait until Monday for the credit approval. I moved into my 2-bedroom apartment in East Point Georgia. It was located 5 minutes from the airport and about 15 minutes from my job.

I never mentioned to my family and friends that my job at Turner was only a 3-month assignment. I believed if I worked within the company somebody there would want to hire me before my time was up. And as God had already predestined it, the former secretary never returned back to work. My supervisor Debbie Monger asked me to fill the position full time and to remain there for a one-year commitment before pursuing other in house opportunities under the Turner umbrella.

As an assistant under Debbie, I gleaned invaluable knowledge. She paid attention to the details, was professional, and had wisdom beyond her years. Debbie personally took me under her wing like Mordecai did Ester. I had favor with her and she made priceless deposits in me by enrolling me in computer classes that increased my worth and afforded me a pay raise. I can think of 5 people who have been instrumental and pivotal in my life, Debbie is one of them.

Debbie worked with efficiency both on the job and as a volunteer. She served the community as a member of the Smyrna Jaycees, an organization that provided opportunities for networking, community involvement and leadership advancement. One day Debbie invited me to a Jaycee meeting and I joined the organization. Being a part of Turner corporate and the Jaycees revealed a way of life I had only dreamed about or seen on TV. I was being exposed to the life-styles of the rich and famous. I was invited to functions and gatherings in honor of the Hawks basketball team. I attended almost every home Hawks game and on occasion sat courtside in the best seats. I also attended the Brave's games and I sometimes sat in the box seats. As members of the Jaycees the Campbell twins and I were able to submit taped auditions for consideration to sing at a Braves game. The Campbell twins were a handsome pair of white young men who could sing and dance. The tape we made singing was reviewed and approved by management of the ball club. We sang the national anthem in 3-part harmony at a Braves home game in the spring of 1989.

Just as I was beginning to think life couldn't get any better, my friends and I began vacationing at Hilton Head Island. One year we even relaxed and dined on one of Ted Turner's islands off the coast of Hilton Head. My friend

Shandle, who had worked with Ted for years, arranged an island tour and meal. It helps to have friends in high places. My childhood best friend and 'play' sister, Shawndra, and about 5 other friends and I spent the entire day in ecstasy aboard his generator run island. The driveway alone was about a mile long. He had a pond filled with piranha fish, and a row of about 10 hammocks on the deck overlooking the beautiful blue waters. This was peaceful living and once I tasted it, I developed an appetite for serenity. From then on I didn't want 10 cars and a mansion, I wanted to own an island. Not a bad goal for a girl from the ghetto.

In Atlanta I was introduced to wealth, independence, community service, and a relationship with God. I joined New Birth Missionary Baptist Church under the leadership of Bishop Eddie Long. It was there that I learned the value of tithing, the wisdom of the word and the simplicity of service. Bishop Long was a servant in a leadership position. He spoon-fed me God's word until I was able to eat without him being present. While at New Birth I was in the choir and a member of the drama ministry. I was a faithful tither and servant so when God opened doors to give me more, I boldly walked through.

I remained loyal on the corporate floor of TBS and was rewarded for my services often and generously. I received a raise every time I acquired a new skill and took on another level of responsibility. When my one-year agreement was up, Debbie, being true to her word, honored my request for an in-house transfer. I began working at CNN/Headline News (HLN) the winter of 1989.

I was originally hired as a Video Journalist but my salary reflected corporate floor compensation so I was quickly trained in another area to justify my high pay status. I worked the graveyard shift as an electronic graphics operator, typing the locations and names of places and people for featured news packages we aired. Thanks to my moms great advice to take typing classes I had found my niche and acquired a little job security.

Again I received an internal nudging. This time it was to seriously pursue acting. I signed with a couple of agents and began auditioning in Atlanta. I landed some extra work on "In the Heat of the Night," and several other TV shows as well as some local plays and film projects. About a month after making the decision to act, I got hired at the Academy Theatre as a tour team member responsible for creating plays for inner city children about inner city challenges - something that I knew about firsthand. I leaped at the opportunity to give back to a community I had come from. The sacrifices I made to participate were spirit-lead because as I reflect back I don't know how I did it.

My typical schedule would include:

9:00a – 5:00p M – F Tour Team Rehearsal @ The Academy
6:00p – 10:00p M – W Sleep @ home
5:30p – 7:00p Th & F Home (shower and change)
7:30p – 10:30p Th – Sat Perform play 'Godspell' @ The Dunwoody
2:30p – 5:30p Sun Perform play 'Godspell' @ The Dunwoody
11:00p – 7:00a Sat – W Work graveyard shift @ HLN
7:30a – 8:45a M – Th Sleep in my car @ Academy (set alarm)
8:45a   M – Th Wake up (15 minutes before rehearsal)
8:45a – 9:00a M – Th Bathroom (brush teeth) for Academy rehearsal

I didn't mind the rigorous schedule. In fact, I was excited about the variety of my days. I was creating plays, singing on stage, and informing a nation via a 24-hour newscast at CNN/Headline News. Life was good. Life was real good. I continued those hours for 2 months straight before the play closed and it was time to tour full time. I had already been approved for a 6-month leave of absence, which began one week prior to my leaving for the tour.

The tour was such a blessing. I was giving back to a community I had survived in. I was dramatizing real life situations by offering assistance to teens on how to handle peer pressure, challenges of growing up in a dysfunctional family, physical abuse and violation, as well as teen pregnancy. All of my life lessons learned up to this point had equipped me to handle questions, address concerns and plant seeds of hope. When the students heard me state I too was raised in the inner city, they realized that anything was possible, including success.

After the tour I returned to CNN/Headline News, the gulf war had broken out. Again my mom's suggestion to take 3 years of typing paid off. I was able to type foreign places and unfamiliar names with speed and accuracy, skills that were greatly appreciated. I worked well under pressure and in intense situations so I became a valuable electronic graphics operator at HLN that year.

However, shortly after the gulf war ended I received another offer to tour the inner city schools again so I requested another LOA. My request was denied because I had previously taken a non-medical LOA. On October 10, 1990 I followed my spirit and decided to resign in order to pursue my dreams. My supervisor at HLN said she would re-hire me if things didn't work out. I had heard that before in Chicago and again I believed it but hoped I would never have to take her up on the offer to return.

A week before rehearsals began for the tour I received a call from the Academy Theatre stating they went in another direction with casting and my services were no longer needed. I was deflated, devastated, and confused. Thank God I had been investing in a 401K plan. I had even increased my deposits to my investment plan to reduce tax penalties associated with working 2 full-time jobs simultaneously. I also had socked a lot into my savings account as a result of working overtime during the gulf war. I eventually had to rely on the funds from my savings account and my 401K to maintain my household expenses. I was constantly seeking God's will and wisdom. I had set what I thought was a realistic goal. I gave myself 6 months to a year to pursue acting before I would have to throw in the towel and return to HLN.

In November, my brother David sent for me to visit him in Boston. Momma's sacrifices paid off, he's a doctor. He invited me to Boston to visit and at the airport on my way back home he gave me a container of dental floss. He said *"Mork"* (the nickname he calls me) *"that's some expensive dental floss you're carrying."* He kissed me on my cheek, we hugged and I boarded the plane. After take off, when it was safe to get up I went into the restroom to examine my 'expensive dental floss' and discovered $3,000 stuffed inside instead of the durable string. It contained $1,000 cash and a $2,000 check. I remember crying in the small bathroom and being grateful for my brother's belief in me. He always tells me *"you inspire me, because you are living your dreams"*.

I returned to Atlanta and shortly afterwards my big break came. I auditioned for the lead role in the film "Babies Coming Home" written and directed by Paula Felder. It was a love story featuring a love scene between a husband and wife. At the time I was cast, I weighed 180lbs so I hired a personal trainer named Antwan Mills to help me create the body I desired to have when I made my film debut. I remember paying him more than I could afford but I believed the change would pay off.

I began a supervised diet and workout routine that enabled me to shed 55lbs. Two months after being cast in the film I showed up for the first rehearsal. The director's jaw dropped and her eyes bugged out as I walked in the door. She immediately asked to speak with me and ushered me to a room in the back of her house and began asking if I was sick. The world had recently become aware of the HIV/AIDS epidemic so I understood her concerns. I informed her of my relentless training schedule to meet my goal of 125lbs for my first lead roll in a film. Paula embraced my new look with great joy.

Unbeknownst to me, my new look added new favor. The windows of heaven were open and pouring me out blessings that continue to drench me to this day. I became a paid professional actor before I completed filming. I booked, several national commercials, 2 stage plays, a dozen industrial films, and 2 Children's TV show pilots that year. I joined both SAG and AFTRA (acting unions) and was making a living doing what I loved to do. I was booked so much as an actor my blessings and bookings lead me back to Chicago.

My move back to my hometown proved to be financially rewarding but spiritually disappointing. I realized being around old buddies brought back old memories and old habits. Atlanta had served as a cleansing and baptizing of sorts. I felt like I had been given a fresh new start to be the best me I could be without pre-judgments. I had been living right and staying out of trouble and it didn't require a lot of effort because I picked the environment I wanted to be in. I had friends who were of a like mind. The people in the circles I traveled in were all doing the same thing - working, going to church, and living a saved lifestyle.

However, when I moved back to Chicago my old stomping grounds, my old ways were in my face once again. I located and joined Apostolic Church of God to continue feeding my spiritual appetite that I had begun satisfying while attending New Birth in Atlanta. However, attending church on Sundays and having daily reminders of the life I used to live, left a way for sin to get in the other 6 days of the week. Prior to leaving Chicago I was known for cursing like a sailor and nearly all my friends used the same language. We were so foul mouthed we called each other B----'s, H---'s and the N--- word when kidding around. We didn't mean any disrespect to one another. We thought we were using the language as a term of endearment. When I think about it now I realize just how lost I was then.

"A Piece of Peace"

Speak Lord…your servant is listening.
- 1 Samuel 3:9

Favor had been prearranged for my arrival. I am so grateful I obeyed. Had I delayed even one day I would have missed a scheduled appointment with my destiny. When God says, "go" or "come" we have to be obedient because we never know what He has planned for us. **At his command he and the entire community of the Israelites will go out, and at his command they will come in." Numbers 27:21b**

We must not allow **FEAR** to override **FAITH** and cause our future to look fuzzy. We do not have to see the land He promised, we just have to believe it exists. Likewise we should not allow what we don't have currently to keep us from getting what He has already given us in eternity. **Faith is the substance of things hoped for and the evidence of things unseen. Hebrews 11:1**

We must listen intently for God's voice and commands. We must be silent when He speaks. Often times we drown out His voice with our own limitations that have been seasoned with another face of distraction. We can't operate in FEAR. We already know **FEAR** is **F**alse **E**vidence **A**ppearing **R**eal but I am writing to further emphasize to you that it is also a **F**ace **E**mbodying **A**nother **R**eality. That other reality is NOT your truth! **FEAR** can cripple you and cause you to stay put when God is clearly calling you to launch out.

I could have stayed where I was, making good money while being close to home, but God had a better plan for me. He wanted me to thirst for Him and learn His character. In order for God to get me thirsty and hungry for Him, He had to remove me from my hometown and reminders of my past. God doesn't do that to everyone, He tailor makes the solution based on the saint and their ability to be obedient. He knows our level of obedience.

God is aware of people and places that pose a threat to our purpose. He's also aware of the other faces of distractions. **Family** and **friends** can take on the form of distraction, not because they're evil or bad but because they know your track record and past mistakes. When God speaks to you He doesn't copy them on the memo. You remember what happened to Joseph when He shared God's vision for he and his brothers don't you? It's easy for someone who knows you to underestimate the power of God's redemptive presence.

I bring you GOoD news! We never have to settle for what others think we can achieve. We can re-invent a wheel already working. People place you inside what they are comfortable in, but we can create options outside of their norm to seek and find what brings God the most pleasure and joy in our lives. Some people will discourage you from doing something different not because it's a bad idea but because of their personal **FEAR** to try something different or risky. Do not fear - be strong and very courageous.

Recognize **FEAR** as a face of **DISTRACTION** and go where **GOD** commands!

Chapter 5

Men on the Mind

Men want respect and women want security.

I woke up thinking about men and I went to sleep meeting them in my dreams. Men were always on my mind. The same could be said for many of my girlfriends. Now you don't have to invite me in, but if I pass by your house please wave yo hand.

After struggling with abandonment issues growing up, I needed and sought validation from men. I wanted to feel valuable, accepted and loved. I became co-dependent. I had a need to be needed. At one point in my life I only dated men that required my help financially, materially or emotionally. I call this type of dating 'personal projects'. The problem was once I fixed or finished the project I didn't want the man anymore.

Then I went through a season of 'type casting' where I only dated men who met a certain type of physical criteria. He had to be fine for me to give him an ounce of my time. In the 80's he had to be light-skinned, in the 90's dark skinned, and no matter what decade we were in he had to be tall. After all, tall men are always in, no matter what season it is. God is still working on me in that area, can I get an amen for tall men!

I even went through a phase of 'give and seek'. I used to give sex and seek love. Sex was a medication to soothe the pain of being alone. If a guy and me were having sex, surely he loved me. If he loved me then I thought he would never leave me. I believed that having sex was as good a guarantee as any that he would always be there. Eventually sex lead to shacking up. The way I saw it was, if I had more clothes at his place than at my apartment we would be better off saving somebody's rent money.

And if we shared the same address I was closer to marriage than most women. I made living with a man a prerequisite for a committed relationship. First we'd live together then one day we *might* get married. I wanted to make sure we were compatible at all times. I justified it by believing that you never really know a person until you live with them and although most people feel that way, it is not how God intended it to work.

I willfully rebelled against Paul's instructions in Romans 12:1. I didn't present my body a living sacrifice, holy and acceptable unto God. Instead I presented my body a *laying* sacrifice, unholy, and unacceptable to God. I fornicated long after I knew it broke the Lord's heart and wasn't His will. I had given my life to the Lord, I just didn't give Him the key to every room. I allowed Him access to my clothes, my money, and my mind. The only room He wasn't allowed to come in was my body or my bedroom.

On top of my hit or miss relationships, I'm a romantic. I don't know if I get it honestly because I'm a poet and a writer or if I completely believe in fairy tales. Either way I love, love. My current DVD collection looks like a romantic requiem. I own 'Bridges over Madison County', 'An Affair to Remember', 'Sleepless in Seattle', ''Pretty Woman, ''The Titanic' and 'Maid in Manhattan.' I really ideally believe I too, can live happily ever after with someone.

However to meet, marry and multiply with "Mr. Right" might take more than my yoyo man diet dating methods I've used in the past. Oh, you've never heard of the yoyo man diet huh? That's when you try every possible diet dating combination hoping one will work. Here's a list of my past misters...

"**Mr. In the Mean Time**" is the man who only got to spend quality time with me while I was waiting for my night in shining armor to show up. Soon as the real deal appeared I quickly went for the upgrade.

"**Mr. Convenient**" was the nice man who always availed himself for a movie, lunch, dinner or a late night conversation no matter how last minute the request was.

"**Mr. Spare Tire**" is who I spent time with when my man wasn't acting right. However, a spare tire was only needed if the original wasn't working properly or when the man I really wanted to see wasn't available.

"**Mr. Validation**" was the man who fit my long laundry list of requirements. He was handsome, charming, articulate and paid. Did I mention he drove a nice car and dressed the part? He was the one who made me feel important and valuable for having the ability to attract and hold his attention.

The challenge with dating a lot of different men at the same time was trying to remember the lies I told to avoid getting caught. It was mentally exhausting creating and recalling stories I'd possibly get questioned on later when they weren't fresh in my mind. That is, until I met a girl name Teresa in Chicago. She was a one man's woman.

Teresa accepted me unconditionally, knew I cursed like a sailor, and hadn't allowed God to fill the void in my heart. She walked with me patiently and non-judgmentally. All she required of me was honesty and she set an example I wanted to emulate. I liked the fact that she never had to screen her words for fear that profanity would flow from her lips. I enjoyed her play by play of a date with her boyfriend that ended in the words "see you tomorrow". She even got me started reading the 'Daily Word'. It's a pocket size biblically based booklet that eventually generated a desire in me to study the book of proverbs in the bible. I read the book of proverbs everyday for almost 5 years.

One day Teresa, Roxanne and I were having breakfast at Wishbone, a down home fish and grits restaurant in Chicago. I was using my predictable colorful language of choice, profanity. All of a sudden I noticed that I was the only one with a limited vocabulary. I stopped eating and paused.

"*Does my cursing bother you?*" I asked.

"*No. That's just the way you are*". Teresa responded. Somewhat satisfied but still wanting validation I asked Roxanne. She very quickly spouted off. "*You've cursed ever since I've known you.*" I continued eating but their answers were now drowning out the sound of me chewing my food. It haunted me. I began to repeat their statements in my mind. That's just the way I am and ever since they have known me I've always cursed. I didn't like that reality so I changed it that day.

I stopped cursing but I knew that stopping a bad habit meant I needed to replace it with a good one. If I didn't put something good in place of it, something worse would creep in. What could I put in the place of profanity? Compliments. I began to speak good things about people and things. I became an encourager.

The next area I needed to get a handle on since my return to Chicago was celibacy. I knew sex before marriage was a sin, but I'd become desensitized to the sin of fornicating until Teresa broke it down by example. I had managed to accomplish the task of celibacy in Atlanta but when I returned to Chicago I started dating an old boyfriend who I'd previously been intimate with so we sort of picked up where we left off. I believe one of the reasons I am still alive and disease free is because I was so terrified of getting pregnant I practiced 'safe sex'. Of course I now know that 'safe sex' is sanctioned sex after marriage.

Teresa burned an image in my mind. She said if my man and me went into my bedroom I should imagine Jesus sitting on my bed. Jesus will stay in the room if we didn't commit a sin. If we started to have sex she said Jesus would not watch the sinful act so either Jesus was going to leave or I needed to ask my man to leave. She then said, "*You don't ever want Jesus to leave your presence.*" I know now that Jesus would never leave me but at the time that image and thought gave me a healthy fear of staying clear of making that choice.

My yoyo diet afforded me some expensive stomach-aches. I've listed 3 of my worst male dating game experiences. My dates and I were destined for destruction. Each of these disasters afforded me some valuable lessons. Literally. Welcome to 'Could this _he_ be Mr. Right?' Is he behind Do' #1 Do' #2 or Do' #3?

Let's start with **Do' #1,** "Northsider". He was tall, handsome, a Christian man, and crazy! He was a compulsive gambler and liar. I was convinced that I could straighten up his life. I believed he just needed a good woman who understood him. I helped him out all right but not before he pawned all of my jewelry on two different occasions, ran up my phone bill and became a fatal attraction whenever I threatened to leave him.

It never occurred to me that I had made myself invaluable and indispensable so there was no way he was going to let this good thing go. Northsider was so crazy he caught the bus from the north side of Chicago to the south side of Chicago wearing a short leather jacket without a scarf, hat or gloves when it was a negative 10 degrees below zero and rang my mother's doorbell at 3 o'clock in the morning looking for me.

Would you like to know the reason for his friendly late night/early morning visit? He was excited. He had finally won enough money to buy back my jewelry he had pawned. I told you he was crazy! Fortunately I began traveling extensively and he got the hint and stopped calling me.

On to **Do' #2** "The Preacher man." We met at a Christians Celibate New Years eve gathering. I was a 'Celibatairre'. He was a preacher (so he said) he had a beautiful Caribbean accent (sometimes) and _knew_ the Word of God (so does satan). By our 3rd date he asked to marry me. I almost said yes. But I decided to put it off till we got to know one another better.

I guess my delay made him a little mad because he decided to stalk my house _and_ me. Shortly after that, he and some of my expensive belongings disappeared. When I called the church to report "Preacher Man," the pastor (of a 20,000 member congregation) _personally_ called me back and said, _"he's not a preacher, several women have reported him and he's an ex-convict who has raped, stolen, and used women. Be very careful,"_ he said. Humm, I counted my $15,000 loss a blessing and praised God for sparing me physical pain.

Last but not least **Do' #3**. He was brilliant with numbers, very conservative _and_ O.C. - Obsessive Compulsive. We had an extremely short courtship before he popped the question, 24 days to be exact. His house was nice and neat. Everything was all lined up. No _everything_. Have you ever seen the movie "Sleeping with the Enemy?" Well, he was like the man in that movie. He couldn't 'concentrate' if anything was turned the wrong way. Towels had to be in a straight row. The labels on bottles had to be lined up and believe it or not, I had to be in order. I couldn't have a hair out of place, a wrinkle in my clothes and Lord forbid I had a bend, a bulge or a big butt. Whew weee he blew a gasket. Remember EVERYTHING had to be lined up, kind of like a spreadsheet.

My ex was an engineer so he liked math & numbers. You know how all the columns and lines have to be perfect on a page? Well the problem was, we humans weren't created to be perfect! But I fell for it and I tried to be his Black Barbie Doll for a while until I realized I had more important things to do. I couldn't be _her_ because I was already great at being me! O.C. had way too much free time on his hands!

"A Piece of Peace"

Men want respect and women want security.

You should know who you are <u>before</u> you DATE someone, not just beginning a journey of self-discovery.

Make sure your mate is confident, secure and aware of their God given **purpose**. It's difficult for a focused man or woman to soar if they are connected to a person who is not motivated or secure with who they are or aware of what they are suppose to do in life. It is also challenging if your mate doesn't have dreams of their own or a sincere desire to support and encourage your dreams.

Men tend to be more visual than women therefore women need to <u>show</u> the men in their lives respect. Men have value and worth and need to be appreciated for their contributions. <u>When a woman speaks down, complains about or rehashes negative things a man has done in the past, without regard to the contributions, adjustments and improvements he has made, it's disrespectful. Men want and need respect.</u> Men were created to be providers and protectors clearly defining their leadership role. When women usurp men's natural ability to do what God purposed them to do it messes with the original intention. Women must visibly and verbally support and nurture the men in their lives. When women do, a man then provides the physical, emotional, spiritual and financial protection that equates to security for women.

<u>Women tend to be more emotional than men therefore men need to help the women in their lives <u>feel</u> secure.</u> Do not shut her out. <u>Communicate, and affirm her.</u> <u>Women want and need security.</u> Women were created to be nurturers and caregivers. When men disregard a woman's natural ability to do what God purposed her to do it puts a strain on the original design. However when a man comes to his woman's defense or provides a place of safety and

53

refuge he helps aid her in feeling more secure. Most women prefer to communicate or check in with their mate periodically. Communication is necessary even if it's difficult. The silent treatment is disrespectful and it leaves the mind to kindle a fire that can cause a back draft. That action actually increases the anxiety associated with a women feeling threatened or insecure.

Both men and women need to speak the truth in love. The truth may hurt but when it's seasoned with love it doesn't sting as bad. When thoughts and emotions are unattended to, time and space fuel them. After while like a fire that has been shut up, it let's out a roar and then it's goal is to destroy everything in sight as it spreads viciously. Two people who love and respect each other will work to respond with godly fruit. **Galatians 5:22-23 But the fruit of the Spirit is love, joy, peace, longsuffering, gentleness, goodness, faith, Meekness, temperance: against such there is no law.**

Women want men to understand them and men want women to view their contributions as valid. Respect and security is key to a successful relationship. If you are with the right person you shouldn't have a challenge implementing these necessary actions.

DATING can be a **DISTRACTION.** Your relationship should be **PURPOSEFUL** and not **PERSONAL** and make sure you and your mate have mapped out a route on the same road. The same direction is important! **Amos 3:3 Can two walk together, except they be agreed?**

Chapter 6

Labor pains

Is there a mid wife in the house?

I was living in LA making a pretty decent living as an actress when I accepted a job to do a national tour of the gospel stage play "Mr. Right Now." Every night fans surrounded us as we signed autographs and took pictures. However, after about 3 weeks into the tour I felt like something was missing. I sought God for a solution. He spoke loud and clear to me one day and gave me a vision.

There was peace in my Spirit and shortly afterwards I began to have 'labor pains' for a spiritual baby. However, giving birth to that idea almost killed me.

I asked God for a vision and He gave me my ministry, the Anointed Agenda, a Christian organizer. It's a daily reminder of God's Word and the practical use of it as inspiration. However being pregnant and giving birth to that baby was the most difficult thing I have ever done in my life. First of all, she was too expensive. Her delivery alone cost about $25,000 dollars! So, I had a little talk with Daddy, it went something like this. "*Yo God, what's up? Why did you give me this bomb digity idea if you knew I couldn't afford to complete it? Where am I supposed to get $25.000 from, huh? Now, I know you're up high and all, but down here on earth money don't grow on trees. Oh I got it Lord maybe you should just drop some manna out of the sky?*"

After I finished talking all crazy to God I heard "charge it." "*I rebuked you in the name of Jesus*". I shouted out loud, "*My God is not a God of debt!*" Then clearly I heard a voice say, "**charge it.**" I knew I heard correctly because I had peace with the command. I found a Christian printer and put $8,000 on my charge card. About a month later the printer called and said they needed to push the deadline back, I said ok, then it happened again. Finally after third delay they said they couldn't complete the job it at all.

I freaked out! I'd been praying and fasting for over 3 weeks and now nothing. *"Excuse me Lord. I know You are my baby's Daddy so what's up? This baby is now in a breach position. Can you turn it around please?"* God did! I got a call from Ester of Print Techniques. She was a *Christian* named Ester. What an appropriate name. It was for such a time as this that she was involved. Well thank God I had a contract and was obedient and charged it because after reviewing the paper work my credit card company put the $8,000 from the original printer in default and I never had to pay it back. Hallelujah!

I eventually gave birth to the books and I was excited because I was a real 'entre-pre-negro'! I immediately called my church to drop off their order, and *my* church informed me that they had purchased two thousand Christian Organizers from *another* company and no longer had plans to purchase mine. I didn't understand that because I had gone through the proper protocol months in advance. I met with the senior pastor, the executive pastor, and the bookstore operator. I wasn't a bench warmer. I was a tither faithfully serving in 3 ministries!

I was at a loss for words and numb, until a friend name Deshon took me to view a mountain on a clear day and said, *"If you have faith the size of a mustard seed, you can tell that mountain right there to move and it will. God can move your books. They're going to do much bigger things for the kingdom than that mountain."* I wept in his arms and understood faith in a personal way that day.

My faith lead me all the way to Arizona. I received a post card in the mail a few days later stating there was a Full Gospel Baptist Conference being held in Phoenix, Arizona. I called my girlfriend Sondra and we loaded up my truck with the Agendas and drove to Arizona that weekend. There were thousands of people in attendance, hundreds of churches, and dozens of pastors and *my baby (The Anointed Agenda)* was being introduced to so many people.

We sold nearly all of the Agendas that weekend. It was a miracle! Only the Lord could take me from an Inglewood, California mentality and give me a United States, no an International vision! My baby is now 5 years old she's in 22 states and 2 countries. Even my home church sells them every year. Remember Jesus could perform no miracles in His hometown! God knew I was thinking too small. He had gifted me a powerful tool for evangelism and I was content with trying to keep it in the family, when His goal was to bless the world.

"A Piece of Peace"

Is there a mid wife in the house?

Please let my spiritual pregnancy become your personal reminder. God desires to trust you with something bigger than yourself. Do not abort the baby inside your spirit no matter how frail it appears, how irregular the heart beat, nor how unlike anyone else's child it seems. God doesn't make any two things identical. If you are carrying a spiritual baby that doesn't look like someone else's baby that's okay as long as it looks like its Father. If you know that God is your baby's Daddy carry it full term.

When giving birth to a vision you need to remember, that seed is subject to attacks. When we co-create with God there is <u>power</u> and <u>purpose</u> inside the <u>package</u>. The power must be protected - that's why you can't share the news of your baby with everyone. When God speaks to you He doesn't use a family telecommunications network to broadcast the vision to your family and friends. News flash, some folks ain't ready for prime time, can't handle the major leagues, and wouldn't know what to do with a St. John ensemble and some matching Jimmy Choo shoes! God tells <u>*you*</u> to do it, not your friends and or family.

It's important to produce or bring forth the vision when it is time. You never want to be out of season with His seed. If He says plant do not plow and if He says till the ground do not reap the harvest. And no matter what you do, do not eat all of your seeds replant some. Sowing a seed ensures another harvest. It is the natural order of things. If you make the ground fertile by tilling it, and then plant and water the seeds, in due season you shall reap. Don't faint and don't be weary, your destiny is just below the dirt. You might not be able to see it, but beyond your view and beneath the surface, Daddy is doing what He purposed.

You do not have to witness a seeds daily growth. Just know that if it is rooted in good soil it will bring forth good fruit. Do not be alarmed if challenges arise and delays appear. They are weeds of **WORRY** that lie in wait. Watch out for **WORRY** another face of **DISTRACTION**. When we **WORRY** our mind searches to solve situations that our sight and intellect can't view or comprehend.

Unfortunately when we can't make sense out of something we think about it all the time. It is as if a tape is repeating over and over in our mind until finally we realize that we have wasted precious time. **WORRY** robs you of the wealth and riches of time. Contrary to popular opinion, time is as valuable as money. But we don't seem to treat it with the same respect. If God gave us money for every minute we lived we would treasure it and treat it with more value.

WORRY actually wastes time because you can't do anything about something that can't be solved without Him. The Word of God says cast all your cares upon Him. The word tells us that His yoke is easy and His burden is light. Why carry the heavy load of **WORRY** when we can put it in the Master's capable hands.

Chapter 7

Blood Tears

The Dirty word spelled with 7 letters.

I'll never forget it. My husband and I sat down and had "the talk" that we'd both been afraid to have. It started off with soft words of reassurance, small doses of what's not working, a pinch of painful anticipation, then a pound of heart break hotel.

Are you familiar with the D word? The one spelled with 7 letters. D-I-V-O-R-C-E. Hum, 7 little letters. Its amazing how 7 letters spoken can change your whole world. 7, isn't it supposed to be the number for completion? Well it was complete all right - completely over. I sat with my eyes full of water attempting to hide the pain. My thoughts took off like a racing horse straight out of a gate to "What now? What went wrong? How can I help this hurt in my heart and these unanswerable questions that keep running through my mind?"

When I let my husband in, I really allowed him access to who I was. I let him see the good, the bad, the ugly, the vulnerable, the courageous, and even the quirky. I peeled off the layers of protection. You know, "the black woman band-aid", and I allowed the bruises, the scars, and the cuts to be exposed. I discovered that <u>air</u> really does heal. But when wounds are wide open like that they're so easily hurt and irritated.

I couldn't help but feel naked when we split. Not because it was a "privilege" for him to have ever been allowed access to me. No, I felt naked because I gave him a piece of me with every conversation, every holding of hands, every gentle kiss, every intimate moment of passion, every discussion turned argument. I gave. I shared, me, willingly and unselfishly to be in tune with and to be together as one.

After we broke up I felt torn, ripped, broken and I didn't know how to put the pieces of my life back together again. I experienced a pain and shame so indescribable until I wanted to lie down, cry, sleep, moan, groan, and scream all at the same time. Because that should not have been happening to me! I was spreading the good news, I wasn't a baby Christian and he was studying to be a minister while in ministerial prep at our church. We both knew the meaning of covenant and commitment. We also knew it broke the Lords heart when Christians divorced. I guess I missed the warning signs. I was his 5th wife! My ex-husband set a new record for 'it's better to marry than to burn'.

The worst part of getting a divorce was the church, not the building but the people inside with the questions. *"How's married life?" Someone would ask.* Nobody knew that I was living in hell at home and I couldn't tell them because they didn't want to hear the real answer. *"Oh, 2 months after we were married my husband told me he made a mistake. I mean, it was the happiest time of my life but he realized he didn't like my hair, my clothes, or my weight. Hum, my husband just didn't like me, so love? Oh, that was definitely out of the question. But enough about me, how are you"?*

On Sunday's alone the public peer pressure would silently suffocate me. It seemed so brutal. It was difficult to mentally manage. I was embarrassed. After all people knew me and knew I was married. All of a sudden I was going to church rollin' solo? So-Low, I felt like I crawled into the sanctuary on Sundays. They would ask, *"Where's your husband"?* I wanted to burst into tears. I wanted him to be with me but he stopped wanting to be by my side. I felt rejected and abandoned all over again like when I was a kid. Even as an adult you never seem to get over the my/daddy/wasn't/home/syndrome.

People had no idea that their questions were like daggers! Each one became a separate, individual blow to my heart and by the time I got to my seat (conveniently located in a back corner somewhere) it was as if a knife had been stabbed, turned, twisted and used to create a zigzag pattern that caused me to wail out in agony audibly!

By the time praise and worship began I was already in tears because I had held back the dam that wanted to flood the aisles for each question I endured. So, I stopped going. Eventually, my daily devotion became an obsession with changing churches. I wanted to go some place where nobody knew me. I wouldn't have to answer questions with a fake façade of *"everything's fine"* reply and no more reminders of where we used to sit together and how we held hands during the entire sermon.

Just dealing with the reality that another relationship had gone wrong was enough! This breaking up business hurts! Why does it have to hurt so bad huh? You just want it to go away. You want it to stop. You want some one to say it ain't so. What am I supposed to do now? I enjoyed cooking for my husband and now I was cooking for a crowd of one. I don't want to be alone for the rest of my life, but I'm so afraid to start all over again to let someone else in. Maybe I should have stopped the divorce process before it got started? Am I now damaged goods? I mean, think about it, after you've been married will anyone else want to marry you? Lets face it…I'm not getting any younger.

Then there's the sight of the sun going down, revealing the empty space and pillow, where my friend, lover, husband once laid. I lie there in my bed alone wishing I could reach on the other side and hold my husband again, tell him I'm sorry, I didn't mean to hurt him and that I forgive him for what he's done and said but I can't. It's too late. I can't go back or erase the tape that's now on an automatic repeat over and over in my mind. So, every day I wake up and I function. I shower, brush my teeth, comb my hair and force myself to eat. Oh, but my mind, my mind takes these mini trips that time can't account for because I don't know how long I've hung in cyberspace contemplating a courtship that crashed in divorce court.

Everyday I have to muster up the energy to let friends and family know that I'm getting better. Everyday I'm getting better. I - am – getting - better. And one day I'll actually believe it. I really will get better but today it doesn't feel good being 'me' apart from him when we were once a 'we'. It feels like, like my eyes are crying blood tears. It's so deep and painful right in the pit of my stomach and all I could do was recite **Romans 8:28 And we know that all things work together for good to them that love God, to them who are the called according to his purpose.**

"A Piece of Peace"

The dirty word spelled with 7 letters.

God wants to get the glory out of marriages. Marriage can work but both people have to work it like a 9-5 and put in overtime daily. If you are being emotionally abused or physically abused please know God does not desire for you to be in danger. Go get help, do not be a helpless hero.

I want you to know that nothing prepares you for divorce or a break up with someone you love. There isn't a book written, a song sang, or poem penned that can accurately assess what a person experiences. I didn't have a clue as to how much pain, shame and disappointment I would endure as a result of it. I was praying and fasting yet I was coming undone. I really believed I would wake up from the nightmare I was having.

When you can't seem to understand something no matter which way you sort it out in your head you get stumped. You stop. I sat stagnate and still at the ledge of unanswered questions. Isn't it interesting when we can't figure something out we think about it ALL the time? No matter which way we turn the thought over in our mind it always ends up at the same place.

We get disappointed or can become depressed. I had no energy and I did the bare necessities. I couldn't write or create anything new for the entire time I was in an emotionally abusive situation. My creativity was cut off because my mind was clogged. I was officially **L.O.S.T.** **L**eaning **O**n **S**cattered **T**houghts.

DEPRESSION is a focus on you instead of giving attention to solving the problem. It is a downward or inward pressing instead of an upward or outward clear focus of the proper view that's needed to clarify or eliminate the problem. During those times we should stop and take stock of what's happening. Locate the problem or challenge. Put all the thoughts, challenges, fears or possible situations out in front of us, either on some paper or record them on a tape. Then read or play them back so we can clearly see or hear how much clutter is consuming our mental space.

DEPRESSION is a face of **DISTRACTION**. The best way to overcome **DEPRESSION** is to pray for peace of mind and find scriptures that support the request. We have to change our view by focusing on what we want to accomplish not what we have or find ourselves doing. It is concentrated effort on clarity, not confusion. Don't hit replay try to record a new more peaceful and productive thought.

Do not go at it alone. Satan wants to single you out, separate you, and seduce you into believing you deserve less than the best. You need to remind Satan that your father has given you a sound mind, a peace that surpasses understanding and He prevents weapons from prospering that have been formed against you.

Our ability to trust God is riding on our ability to locate His presence. We can't when we are overly consumed with negative thoughts that keep changing stations in our minds. We must learn the lesson even from events that hurt or wound us. When we do we can share them in honesty, and heal from them emotionally. God's design for our destiny is not without its share of detours. Don't get L.O.S.T. along the way!

I am excited! After a year of absence, I pray I now write clearer, more honestly, and much more personally than I have ever penned prior to this point in my life. Today, I gladly press keys and bend knees because I can speak boldly about being pruned. It's worth the pain of purpose!

Chapter 8

In 2 me C

Intimacy with God – my time with Him.

To take a closer more intimate look at my internal make up I've used the last few pages to share some practical spiritual practices I have implemented to gain and remain focused. These phrases and analogies serve as guardrails for my walk with God. I minister all over the world and most people only witness the external successes God has given me. Very few people have an accurate assessment of what I went through to land on my knees.

Hopefully these examples will help you handle your challenging circumstances. Whether your situation is similar in nature to mine or a totally different test or trial, I believe we can benefit from believers who aren't afraid to show their bruises! Take the band-aid off and allow the air to heal your hurts. Praying, praising, and prose have become my solace. I want to thank you for allowing me to sit and sup with you and for taking in my souls prose. I pray this deposit yields a lofty return and remember I don't want no change back!

Learn from life's test and live "BEYOND BLESSED!"

On praying. At one time praying daily was difficult for me to do. I was so easily distracted. The telephone, my chores, the computer, or my desire to write became daily distractions. Other times I would end up daydreaming or thinking about bills, my to do list, or relationships. Sometimes I would even get on my knees to pray and fall asleep. It was as if a dozing demon or sleep servant would seduce me into a deep slumber when I kneeled down to pray to God. I used to feel horrible when that happened.

Until one day I fought back. I refused to fall asleep on the Father again. I was angry with myself for disrespecting God and His valuable time. That day I grabbed my journal off the nightstand and I began to write an apology to God. I wrote down how I felt and how sorry I was for sleeping on the job.

When I read the words on the paper I realized that my thoughts were uncensored, unedited, and without interruption. The pages revealed something pure, personal, and purposeful. For the first time in my walk with God I realized that my prayers or conversations with God could be penned.

It was an epiphany! I enjoyed communicating with words on paper just as much as spoken words. I also realized when I wrote what I felt on the inside I didn't have to be "spiritually correct" - I just had to be honest. I understood that God already knew my heart, I was the one who didn't know it. Now when I write my prayers to God I have an opportunity to look back and locate the space I was in when I shared and asked certain things or what frame of mind I had at the time.

I realized not only were my thoughts on paper pure but also the pages were readily available to be used. In order to pray I needed a clean canvas. I didn't know that I couldn't kneel down to pray without first clearing my mind. I had to clear away the clutter. I didn't erase what was on my mind. I put my thoughts in perspective. I needed to direct my attention to the man of the hour, God. My penned prayers are some of the most personal things that have ever crossed my mind or been entertained in my heart.

After learning how to pray to God on paper I had to **practice praying** to Him on my knees again. Yes, I practiced. I started off consecrating 5 minutes of consistent prayer time and then I gradually moved up to 45 minutes to an hour. I took baby steps back to my knees. I refused to get overwhelmed with trying to calculate the quantity of time with Him without first working on the quality of time we had. If I only spend five minutes with Him they are the most intimate minutes of my day.

On praising. I have tried to analyze my praise time with Daddy. I use to think of praising God only when I was in church service and everyone lifted their hands to sing songs to God. I didn't realize until much later in my relationship with God that praising Him was more than a Sunday morning experience, it is an every morning experience.

I tried to stand in my bedroom and say hallelujah out loud while clapping my hands but it felt forced and mechanical. I then tried to remember every praise song my church choir sung but that didn't seem sincere. So I started putting on music by Yolanda Adams or Brent Jones and the TP mob. I would hit repeat on my stereo to hear *"Thank You Jesus"* by Brent or *"Let Us Worship Him"* by Yolanda and the next thing I knew I'd be in praise mode, crying tears of joy and thanksgiving.

However, I really learned to praise God on paper. I would pen everything that I could think of that He did for me. I would pen the physical, mental, emotional, spiritual, and material blessings He provided. I would pen the blessing of salvation, inheritance, and acceptance. I'd write about His mercy, grace, forgiveness, love, safety, and the blessings I wasn't even aware He handled. The next thing I knew, my hands would be aching and my wrist would be in pain before I'd realized that there were too many blessings to write about. Thank you Father, Hallelujah!

So I started singing and speaking my praises to God. Eventually I worked up to praising God minus the music but with a song in my heart. I still sing to Him when I praise Him but it's no longer a prerequisite to begin. I started with a simple thank you Father and then I think of all He has done on just that morning. Within a minute I would be in full praise because I'd get overwhelmed with the reality of how much He had done even in just one second. When I would enter into His presence it would be so peaceful and power-FULL that I didn't ever want to leave.

Then I had an 'Aha moment', as Oprah Winfrey would say. I couldn't get it all out in a morning praise session or even an evening praise session. **I had to live a life of constant and consistent praise.** Just then it hit me - I have to be in praise mode every second, minute, hour, and day of my life. When I wake up, leave the house, get a booking on a show, or get secured to speak at a church, I've got to praise Him. When I get a parking ticket, cut off on the freeway, passed over for a TV show, I've got to praise Him. When a friend or loved one goes through a difficult situation or I have a challenging time in a relationship I still have to praise Him.

I learned that every opportunity I have to experience God's providential hand working on my behalf is an occasion worth acknowledging! After all, God is the giver of life and love, so that means that the lessons learned are an extension of His earnest desire to create character in me. **God is so incredibly full and fulfilling that He allows us to get filled with the fruit of the spirit to share the seeds of sweetness with someone else.** That's awesome!

He allows us to digest disappointments in order to create detours to prevent another person's demise. God delights in us telling our tests, trials, and testimonies we've experienced so we can teach someone about His goodness. God is concerned with our worship in spite of our worries. He wants to know we believe our expectations are second to His destination. Our daily steps are deliberately and intentionally ordered to lead us on our path to purpose. **Psalm 119:133 Order my steps in thy word: and let not any iniquity have dominion over me.**

<u>**My Prose.**</u> I keep a journal by my bed. I realized that my thoughts and concerns of the day needed to be somewhere other than crowded inside my mind. I needed to purge and free up some space to create. Yes, create! I now write down life lessons I've learned. I discovered that my stories and experiences are not as unique as I once thought they were. I realized that other folks have survived the same or similar

settings, set backs and set ups as me. I share my prose in my spoken word music.I display my stories in performance poetry engagements. I dramatize it on stage and in plays emphasizing it's power, impact and effect. I publish poems and short stories to help people who I may never come in contact with, understand this journey called life a little better. My Prose is an important piece of a puzzle that now has a place. The power of a pen, the patience of poet awaiting the proper word to use, and the peace of a person who has truly put her trust in God.

"A Piece of Peace"

Intimacy with God...my time with Him.

As a result of my varied experiences, I have learned to trust God in spite of what my situation looks like. I have a heightened faith in my Father's ability to fulfill the truth of His Word. I created some acronyms and phrases to assist me along my journey.

Purpose has a face and you can prepare by placing visual reminders in front of you to guide and direct your steps. Your steps are ordered by the Lord, so make sure you know what the manual says about where you are going and what you are building.

I hope they inspire, encourage and equip you with practical ways to see yourself and situation from God view!

Make sure you **T.R.O.B**.
Trust the Word of God.
Read the Word of God.
Obey the Word of God.
Believe the Word of God.

If you do not **TROB** you will probably to get into **TROUBLE!**

If God said it then it is! Daily I work on building my confidence and boldness in His promises. They push me when I want to stop and pull me when I can't find the footing to move forward. I still get discouraged some times but the difference in how I react is credited to what I call **Q.R.T. Quick Recovery Time**. How quickly can I recover from an adverse situation? Unexpected challenges will arise and disappointing moments will occur, however how we handle our storms is a direct indication of our maturity in Him.

Make up your mind to take back your time. Things that take an hour to get over we should work on decreasing their ability to delay our day. Our reaction to a disappointment shouldn't rob us of our chance to witness to someone. We can't let the frustration of a moment hold us hostage in our head or keep our time captive.

There isn't anything that can over take us and there is no temptation that's too difficult for God to guide us out of. We should not be blown over each and every time something disappointing or challenging happens. Nor should we throw in the towel when the water gets a little high. If you realize you are in an overflowing bathtub find a way to pull the plug and let some of the water out. If you are in the deep end of a pool look for a ledge to lift yourself up then take a deep breath before going back in. Do not allow problems and set backs to paralyze you - use them to propel you forward.

We humans have something no other creature on earth has. I call it '**Pause-ability**.' Unlike a dog, cat, or any other animal for that matter we have a built in mechanism called 'reason.' Humans have the ability to reason, pause, or make sense out of a situation prior to reacting. If you step on a dog's tail he might snap or bite you without realizing it was an accident. However, we have the opportunity to process an action before choosing our reaction. When someone does or says something to you that you dislike, don't snap or bite their head off. Exercise **pause-ability** and process the proper response. You might want to do what I do sometimes. I pray that I can keep my mouth shut until the Holy Spirit gives me <u>kind</u> words to speak.

The One Touch Rule. When a bill comes in I open it, write out the check and mail it off. The One Touch Rule can help you to become debt free or at least stress free financially. I don't wait for the due date to arrive. I pay bills immediately. If you want to implement the **One Touch Rule** I suggest you start with something small like a gas bill or electric bill and pay it as soon as you receive it. Then work up to the car note or mortgage payment. If you only pay bills (give) on the 1st and the 15th you are basically creating an opening to receive only 2x's a month. **Romans**

13:8 Let no debt remain outstanding, except the continuing debt to love one another, for he who loves his fellowman has fulfilled the law. If you borrowed money from a friend when you had money in your possession hopefully you would repay them. Well, the same works with your bills. When you get the money pay your bills. You do not have to wait until a due date arrives. You should try the **One Touch Rule** I believe you will be surprised at the freedom there is in giving. A great thing about giving is, you set yourself up to receive! Who knows you might even find that you are no longer living paycheck to paycheck because you are creating a constant flow for your finances. Don't block your blessings by clogging your cash flow!

Beeeeeeeeeeeep. The next time you receive unfair treatment or you find yourself in a delayed or challenging situation, hit the mute button in your mind and say to yourself **beeeeeeeeeeeep** this is a test, this is only a test and at the end of the test I will have a testimony. Then shout hallelujah when it's over. It works for me. God is watching how we react; we should work hard to pass His test.

Beware of **VISION BLOCKERS.** These are people who can't see what God has shown you so they attempt to stand in your way. Take note of people you talk to that have the ability to cause you to stumble while walking in the footsteps of faith. If you have appointed someone to a purposeful position in your life make sure they are worthy of the responsibility that comes along with that promotion. We have placed or created a false sense of security in some friends and family member. We have misled them about who they are to us. They are not our Lord or leader, in most cases they are just people with an opinion.

Who has the ability to influence your mind by reminding you of a mistake you made in your past? (i.e. it didn't work then why will it work now). You must disconnect the plug that gives them the power to push the play button to your past. You have to demote some folks. Some folks need to be demoted to **COACH CLASS** in your life...not everyone is worthy of riding in a **FIRST CLASS, PRIORITY SEAT** in your life.

Please understand, you cannot argue, disagree or get frustrated with someone you have appointed to a leadership role in your life based on familiarity and time. You have to uproot and stop their source of strength in your life.

The people you've put in charge need to be qualified to speak into you life, not appointed by default. That goes for co-workers, family members, ex-boyfriends and sista friends who have known you almost all your life. Do not get his confused with those who are appointed to speak into your life and are qualified to counsel you or have been positined to be an accountability partner.

Ask yourself those four simple truths I shared with you earlier if you plan to give anyone authority to deposit into your life. Do they T.R.O.B.? When you commit to this process your view will be sharpened, your discernment will be clearer which means you will be more available to hear His voice and His will. Make sure they **TROB**. How can anyone who doesn't know what God's Word says about a situation offer you godly advice? At best they can give you an opinion but opinions we know are like butt holes everybody has one. You have to have a firmer foundation than that.

Maura-isms

M.O.M. - Mind over matter – Focused attention on what you want to happen, manifest or materialize instead of allowing the monster in your mind to render you helpless or hopeless. We've all heard or read the phrase objects in mirror appear larger well, **"Objects in your mind appear larger than in real life."**

EXERCISE:
To create clarity from chaos write your worries in word form onto a piece of paper and SEE how little they actually are.
"The actual size of your problem is not as big as the monster you've created in your mind".

No Negative Near – get rid of what gets you.
Know which people feed and fuel you by making a list of 10 people. Which friends give and which friends take. If you are down or empty know which calls you can take and which calls to make. Know which people dump and drain you and which ones build and fill you.

FX - Finding your X-Factor – What do you have to offer this world? How can that gift, talent, or skill best be utilized? Everyone was created uniquely and differently for a reason find out why God allowed you to survive the other millions of sperms that didn't make it.

Weighty Words – Your words have weight they either build people up or break people down. We must choose our words carefully since there is power in our words.

EXAMPLE:
When was the last time you made this statement?
I can KILL 2 BIRDS with 1 STONE

Not only do we say we will kill some innocent birds but we are going to kill them with a stone. Doesn't that sound painful?

Here is a more positive way to accomplish the same task.
I can BLESS 2 ANGELS with 1 KISS
Not only do we get a chance to bless an angel but we can also pucker up for something positive. Doesn't that sound pleasing?

How many times have you made this statement?
I FELL in love or I'm FALLING in love?
Let's break down fell and fall.
Last time I checked no one likes to fall. It isn't good to have an impending end. No one wants to hit the concrete, the floor or fall down some stairs or into someone else. That is usually a BAD or UNCOMFORTABLE thing.

Try this phrase instead...
I ASCENDED into love or I'm RISING into love
How high do you want to go? Try to touch the sky!

About the Vessel

Maura Gale is a speaker actress, poet and author of the **Anointed Agenda**™(a Christian Organizer). She co-produced the stage play **"STEM"** and recently co-produced the film **StemTheMovement,** a DocuDramady of 3 women's courageous journeys through life. As an evangelist Maura hosts, performs poetry and shares her one woman show **"She Speaks"** at conferences, retreats, concerts, fashion shows, and special events around the world. Maura is a celebrated poet and recording artist. She has released 2 Spoken Words CD's and is currently in the studio working on a follow up project **"MAURA"** to be released soon.

As an actress, you've seen her in the ABC movie of the week **"Their Eyes Were Watching God"** produced by Harpo Films/Oprah Winfrey. Other credits include **Strong Medicine"**, **"NYPD Blue"**, **"Ally McBeal"**, **"City of Angels"** or as Claudia the lead role in **"Love and Fate"** on Starz, Encore and BET. Her most popular stage credits include The Steppinwold Theater's **"For Colored Girls who have…** and **"Mr. Right Now."** She has over 100 radio and TV commercials to her credit and is a National Spokesperson for several Fortune 500 Companies speaking to over a million people yearly.

She has shared the stage with some anointed people: Kim Stratton, Donnie McClurkin, Mary Mary, Vicki Winans, Be Be Winans, Donald Lawrence, Karen Clark Sheard, Jonathan Slocumb and Vanessa Bell Calloway.

Maura Gale has performed **personalized** poetry for: *Black Caucus*, *NAACP-The Rosa Parks Story, NY Clergy Men*, Pentecostal Assemblies of the World - *Bishop's Dinner Cruise, Miss and Ms. Black California Pageant, 100 Black Men Organization, Inglewood and Compton Mayors Office,* and her signature piece "Love Grows" was written for *"Save our Future"* an *Essence* Award Recipient.

Order Form

Name:		
Address:		
City:		State:
Zip Code:		
Day Telephone:		
Quantity x $10.00 per book		
Subtotal		
Sales Tax (CA add 8.25% per book)		
Shipping and Handling		
	1 Book add $5.50	
	2 Books add $7.50	
	3+ Add $2.00 per add.l book after 2	
Total Amount Due		
MAKE CHECKS OR MONEY ORDERS PAYABLE TO: **Maura Gale** PO Box 366001 Atlanta, GA 30336 310-358-3398		

Request books via c-mail: info@mauragale.com

Other products and services
by Maura Gale

The Anointed Agenda™ - Christian Organizer
(Available October of every year)

Ear Candy - Spoken Word CD
(Live poetry performance with music)

Ride Rosa Ride CD (single)
(Rosa Parks Poetic journey to purpose)

STEMtheMovement – DocuDramady Film
(3 Women's share on film transparently, life experiences)
www.StemTheMovement.org #StemTheMovement

She Speaks – Series of One Woman Shows
(Women of the Word are seen and heard on stage)

Visit website for more details
www.mauragale.com
Connect on Social Media @MauraGale

To contact the author regarding speaking engagements, mistress of ceremony, seminars and poetic performances for church, conferences, retreats, the school system or your special event please send written request to the above web address or e-mail info@mauragale.com

Brenda J. Jones
20 Redondo Street
San Francisco, CA   94124-3539